CAN'T MISS™
flower
GARDENING

Practical Solutions for Gardening Success

Published by Cool Springs Press, a Division of Thomas Nelson, Inc., P.O. Box 141000, Nashville, Tennessee 37214.

Dunn, Teri.
    Can't miss flower gardening : practical solutions for gardening
    success / Teri Dunn.
      p. cm.
    Includes bibliographical references and index.
    ISBN: 1-59186-157-8
    1. Flower gardening. I. Title.
  SB405.D86 2005
  635.9–dc22

                         2004025084

First printing 2005
Printed in the United States of America
10 9 8 7 6 5 4 3 2 1

Managing Editor: Jenny Andrews
Copyeditor: Sara J. Henry
Cover Design: Becky Brawner, Unlikely Suburban Design
Book Design: Bruce Gore
Production Artist: S.E. Anderson
Cover Photo: David Winger

Cool Springs Press books may be purchased in bulk for educational, business, fundraising, or sales promotional use. For information, please email SpecialMarkets@ThomasNelson.com.

Visit the Thomas Nelson website at **www.ThomasNelson.com** and the Cool Springs Press website at **www.coolspringspress.net.**

CAN'T MISS™
flower
GARDENING

Practical Solutions for Gardening Success

Teri Dunn

COOL SPRINGS PRESS
A Division of Thomas Nelson Publishers
Since 1798

acknowledgements

Many thanks to: Jenny Andrews and Hank McBride, Nancy Reid, Brian and Mimi, Foley for Buddy, Wasis Diop, Lynette Gaslin ... *y los tres amigos.*

—Teri Dunn

photo credits

contents

introduction

Color Your World
with Flowers

most of us probably have long forgotten the first time we pressed our nose into a flower or knelt to study its remarkable form. Sometimes it takes watching someone else respond to a flower—witnessing a small child filled with wonder or a mother or sweetheart savoring a bouquet—to appreciate it anew. Suddenly all the delight comes flooding back, for there are few things on earth as enchanting and as beautiful as flowers.

The first step in successful flower gardening is simply to choose plants wisely.

Growing your own flowers is a unique thrill. You choose, plant, nurture, watch, hope, and one fine day, the flowers appear. You are torn between cutting them immediately for a bouquet or sparing them so they can beautify your yard. As restless and enamored as a nectar-seeking bee or hummingbird, you walk through your garden over and over again to admire the flowers.

When you grow your own flowers, whether annuals, perennials, bulbs, shrubs, vines, or small ornamental trees, you want them to bloom profusely, last a long time, and look as good as possible. For that kind of success, there are many "tricks of the trade," which you will find in the chapters that follow. But the first step in successful flower gardening is simply to choose plants wisely. Select those that are known to thrive in your region and in the particular sun and soil conditions of your yard. To that end, we have included a gallery of Can't Miss Flowers in the latter part of this book, complete with information on each plant's requirements and its special features.

Filling your garden, and your life, with beautiful flowers is absolutely an attainable goal. And when you do, you find that the joy and satisfaction of having them around—outdoors in the garden as well as indoors in bouquets—changes your life. Flower gardening is more than a hobby; it is a happy decision to fill your world with the simple and delicious pleasures of color and fragrance and beauty.

Top: *Sedum kamtschaticum*
Center: *Nicotiana alata*
Bottom: *Veronica peduncularis*

The Garden "Canvas"

It is a great pleasure to create a design in your garden with flowers. To begin, it helps to think of your entire yard as a big, blank canvas, or at least to see certain areas as open opportunities—and to think of the plants as the paints. This is the reason professional garden designers often refer to the plant "palette." Every color of the rainbow, every form imaginable is available to you—which makes the composition possibilities many and exciting!

But designing a garden can also be a bit intimidating, especially if you want to approach it like a landscape professional. Sometimes those folks seem to be speaking another language, referring to "placement of plant

Growing beautiful flowers is one of the greatest joys of gardening.

materials," "color harmonies," "vignettes," and so forth—and they seem to expect complete control over the results.

Let's not forget that even with the best-laid plans, plants are simply not static and obedient and completely predictable. Hues, heights, and blooming times can vary. A plant may not grow well in the spot you've assigned it or may decide on its own to sprout and thrive in some other part of your yard. Or you may discover a gorgeous combination quite by accident, as when gathering flowers for a bouquet and realizing that if two plants look great in a flower arrangement, they would also look terrific growing adjacent to one another.

To "design" a flower garden, you need to have good, well-thought-out ideas—the chapters ahead will show you plenty of these and guide you through them. But it also helps to remain flexible and open to the surprises and vagaries of nature. The good news is that the natural exuberance and variability of well-grown flowers lets you experiment. In a garden you can make changes, move things around, make new "pictures," and improve others.

In that sense, gardeners have it easier than painters. Revisions and refinements are not a serious hurdle. In fact, the process itself is fun and rewarding. Over time, you are sure to arrive at flower borders, arrangements, or small scenes that really please you. And you can look forward to many more, with each passing year, as your knowledge and "palette" increase. Bear in mind, too, that plant breeders and flower nurseries will continue to introduce tempting new and improved plants for you to consider and perhaps fall in love with and add to your landscape. A flower garden is truly, always a living, vibrant work in progress. You will irresistibly become involved and absorbed—and your own creativity is sure to blossom!

Plant breeders have answered our call for more compact, more floriferous plants that give us maximum "bang for the buck"—plants that fill any garden, even smaller ones, with bountiful color. At the same time, many of today's most popular plants are also less work. Disease resistance has been fostered, and anything with very fussy soil or care requirements is not as commonly grown. So we want, we need—and we get—easier, more attractive, more productive plants. The plant choices today are far greater than they were in times long past, or even just ten or twenty years ago.

Getting Started

The best place to start planning your flower garden—and the way to assure success right from the start—is to match the plants you choose to your site. This approach saves you from backbreaking alterations (such as removing trees to force a sunny garden or digging up a big area and filling it with new soil) and endless maintenance chores. If you have a sunny spot, shop for sun-loving plants; if you have an area of damp ground, plant it with moisture-lovers. And so forth.

There are a wide variety of approaches. You can grow butterfly-attracting plants, create an old-fashioned-looking cottage garden, or install a formal bed. If you don't want to keep plundering your displays to make bouquets, you can set up a special area as a cutting garden. Whatever you decide, don't be bound by ideas of a "finished" product or a "perfect" garden. Life is busy, and you ought to have a garden you can be proud of and truly enjoy. Aim for beautiful designs that are basic and attainable, which can be accomplished in average situations. Let this book guide and inspire you as you work toward the flower garden of your dreams.

CAN'T MISS TIP:

THE FIVE KEYS TO SUCCESS

Flower gardening is easy when you stick to the basics:

- Good soil
- The right amount of light
- A little plant food to boost flower-bud production
- Enough water at the right times
- Deadheading of spent flowers, to encourage more growth

The world of flower gardening offers many exciting (and easy to grow) possibilities.

So Many Choices

Setting out to make a flower garden is a great adventure. There's anticipation—how will it look if I try *this?* There's planning—studying your options and arriving at a design. There's mystery—seeing and marveling at what thrives or looks wonderful. There's work—digging, getting down on your hands and knees, and then later tending to the plants. And yes, there's awe—witnessing ever-changing beauty, every day!

So it bears learning as much as you can about flowers as you set out. That way, you can make informed choices. Everything you discover about a plant will not only broaden your appreciation of it, but will inspire and enable you to make the most of its qualities. As you consider the many, many choices available to you, narrow your search to the flowers you really want to grow. The idea is to draw from a broad "palette" so you have the most interesting and satisfying garden possible. And realize that nothing is forever! You can alter your garden a bit each season, or completely redesign it. If you choose to forgo a tempting plant now, promise yourself you will find a way to try it later.

One way to start choosing plants for your flower displays is to consider such characteristics as color, texture, form, and height. For instance, a wish for red flowers might lead you to geraniums, salvias, or dahlias, or a desire for tall, spiky perennials might point you toward blazing star, red-hot poker, or delphinium. Of course there's more to each of these than their appearance—bloom time and growing requirements may keep them on your wish list or eliminate them. But it's a place to begin, and it helps you narrow the options.

Flowers can be found in every color imaginable, and can be used to give a garden energy or tranquility.

A Rainbow of Choices

Perhaps the greatest delight we get from our flower gardens is color. Literally every hue in the rainbow is available, as well as white and green. There are even near-black flowers (such as the hollyhock called 'Nigra', and a hybrid tea rose called 'Taboo'). If you really like a certain color or it goes well with your house or trim, you can find myriad possibilities and hue variations among a vast array of beautiful annuals, perennials, flowering bulbs, vines, shrubs, and trees.

Certain colors seem to establish certain moods. Flower color can also help create balance within your garden's conditions and layout. The best way to get a handle on color in your garden—and to clarify your taste or style—is to study color relationships. Look carefully at other people's gardens; ponder bouquets that you admire; and browse the photos in this book, other gardening books, and gardening magazines. More information on flower color can be found in Chapter 3. To get some idea of the vast array of flowers available within each color, see the lists on the following pages.

Everything you discover about a plant will not only broaden your appreciation of it, but will inspire and enable you to make the most of its qualities.

Flowering plants come in a full range of rainbow colors, and placing and combining colors can be the most exciting part of gardening. The following are only short lists. There are many more varieties available, and plant breeders are continually adding to the selection.

Lilium lancifolium

Feisty Reds

For best results, use red (and hot pink) sparingly in mixed-color flower beds, as a little bit goes a long way. And don't forget: Hummingbirds adore red flowers.

Bee Balm (*Monarda didyma*): 'Gardenview Scarlet'

Canna (*Canna × generalis*): 'Australia', 'Endeavor', 'President'

Crocosmia (*Crocosmia* hybrids): 'Lucifer'

Pinks (*Dianthus* species and cultivars): 'Hoffman's Red', 'Ian', 'Zing Rose'

Poppy (*Papaver orientale*): 'Bonfire', 'Glowing Embers'

Rhododendron (*Rhododendron* species and cultivars): 'Besse Howells', 'Hellikki', 'Nova Zembla'

Salvia (*Salvia* species): 'Salsa', 'Lady in Red'

Summer Phlox (*Phlox paniculata*): 'Starfire'

Tulip (*Tulipa* hybrids and species): 'Kingsblood', 'Red Emperor'

Weigela (*Weigela florida*): 'Red Prince'

Bright Oranges

Orange is a cheerful flower color, welcome in sunny spots. Though in the pastel-dominated gardens of years ago it was considered a difficult color to work with, orange has become a popular flower color. The recent trend is to combine it with purple or blue flowers, in a flower bed or in a pot display, or mixed with white and yellow.

Azalea (*Rhododendron* hybrids): 'Mandarin Lights' (deciduous), 'Girard Hot Shot' (evergreen)

Butterfly Weed (*Asclepias tuberosa*)

California Poppy (*Eschscholzia californica*)

Cosmos (*Cosmos sulphureus*): 'Cosmic Orange'

Lily (*Lilium* species): *Lilium lancifolium*, *Lilium henryi*, Asiatic Lilies 'Apeldoorn' and 'Tropical Dream'

Nasturtium (*Tropaeolum majus*)

Poppy (*Papaver orientale*): 'Midnight', 'Turkenlouis'

Potentilla (*Potentilla fruticosa*): 'Sunset'

Red Hot Poker (*Kniphofia uvaria*): 'Bressingham Comet', 'Drummore Apricot'

Trumpet Vine (*Campsis radicans*)

Zinnia (*Zinnia elegans*): 'Profusion Orange'

Sunny Yellows

Radiant and fresh even on hot summer days, yellow is an important part of any flower display. Bright enough to join bold-color areas, it can also be used to brighten pastel-themed beds.

Annual Sunflower (*Helianthus annuus*)

Black-Eyed Susan Vine (*Thunbergia alata*)

Coreopsis (*Coreopsis verticillata*)

Daylily (*Hemerocallis* hybrids): 'Stella d'Oro', 'Happy Returns'

Evening Primrose (*Oenothera fruticosa*)

Forsythia (*Forsythia × intermedia*)

Kerria (*Kerria japonica*)

Lily (*Lilium* species and cultivars): Asiatic 'Connecticut King', Oriental 'Golden Star Gazer'

Perennial Sunflower (*Helianthus × multiflorus*)

St. John's Wort (*Hypericum* species)

Pretty Pinks

Romantic or perky, pink is always a lovely sight in flower gardens. It is especially striking with dark blue, purple, and deeper pinks. Pastel pink is less successful with yellow, unless you are making a sort of "Easter-egg colors" display that also includes some softer yellow and lavender flowers of similar intensity.

Aster (*Aster* species and cultivars): 'Alma Potschke', 'Harrington's Pink'

Foxglove (*Digitalis purpurea*)

Japanese Anemone (*Anemone × hybrida*): 'Bressingham Glow', 'Queen Charlotte'

Peony (*Paeonia lactiflora*): 'Monsieur Jules Elie', 'Sorbet'

Pink (*Dianthus* species and cultivars): 'Bath's Pink', 'Betty Morton'

Poppy (*Papaver orientale*): 'Juliana'

Rhododendron (*Rhododendron* species and cultivars): 'April Rose', 'English Roseum', 'Yaku Princess'

Rock Rose (*Cistus* hybrids): 'Barnsley Pink'

Rose (*Rosa* species and cultivars): grandiflora 'Queen Elizabeth', single-flowered floribunda 'Betty Prior', English 'Abraham Darby'

Summer Phlox (*Phlox paniculata*): 'Sir John Falstaff, 'Tracy's Treasure'

Lovely Lavenders

Flowers in all shades of light and dark purple are fabulous in association with one another, in borders as well as a vase. When you pair purple with yellow, however, it is drawn out of the shadows and delights the eye.

California Lilac (*Ceanothus* species and hybrids): 'Dark Star', 'Julia Phelps'

Catmint (*Nepeta* × *faassenii*)

Hyacinth (*Hyacinthus orientalis*)

Impatiens (*Impatiens walleriana*): 'Blue Pearl'

Lavender (*Lavandula* species and cultivars)

Lilac (*Syringa vulgaris* and others): 'Katherine Havemeyer', 'Miss Kim'

Petunia (*Petunia* × *hybrida*): 'Lavender Wave', 'Limbo Violet'

True Blues

Cool blue hues seem to fit with almost any other flower color, but they are especially wonderful with lemon yellow or bright pink. Blue also has a stabilizing effect when combined with hot, bold colors.

Bachelor's Button (*Centaurea cyanus*): 'Blue Boy'

Bellflower (*Campanula* species): 'Blue Clips'

Clematis (*Clematis* species and cultivars): 'General Sikorski', 'Will Goodwin'

Delphinium (*Delphinium elatum*): 'Blue Lace', 'Summer Skies'

Flax (*Linum perenne*)

Forget-Me-Not (*Myosotis* species)

Geranium (*Geranium* species and hybrids): 'Johnson's Blue', 'Boone'

Grape Hyacinth (*Muscari armeniacum*)

Hydrangea (*Hydrangea macrophylla* and hybrids): 'Blue Wave', 'Endless Summer', 'Nikko Blue', 'Dooley'

Morning Glory (*Ipomoea tricolor*): 'Heavenly Blue'

Veronica (*Veronica peduncularis*): 'Georgia Blue'

Soft Yellows and Creams

Mix these soft flowers with pastel pink, lavender, or darker yellow, or pair them with blue or purple flowers (in the garden or vase) for an elegant look.

Broom (*Cytisus* × *praecox*)

Daffodil (*Narcissus* species and cultivars)

Daylily (*Hemerocallis* cultivars): 'Joan Senior', 'Quietly Awesome'

Foxglove (*Digitalis lutea*)

Lily (*Lilium* species and cultivars): Oriental 'Muscadet'

Lucky Limes

These gentle hues can give your flower garden a boost of sophistication, especially when combined with red or deep purple flowers.

Flowering Tobacco (*Nicotiana* × *sanderae*): 'Lime Green'

Lady's Mantle (*Alchemilla mollis*)

Spurge (*Euphorbia* species)

Zinnia (*Zinnia elegans*):'Envy'

Night Lights: Pure White Favorites

The evening hours are the perfect time to relax outdoors, especially if you've been away all day at work or school. Numerous white flowers are at their best and most glowing then, radiating a sense of peace and coolness over the yard even as their sweet scents attract night-flying pollinators (not all are fragrant, but many are). So if this is the time of day when you savor your yard, group or emphasize white or light-colored flowers—by the patio, deck, or hammock, or wherever you like to linger as the day slows down and the moon rises.

Baby's Breath (*Gypsophila paniculata*)

Bellflower (*Campanula* species): 'White Clips', 'Alba'

Blazing Star (*Liatris spicata*): 'Floristan White'

Bridal Wreath Spirea (*Spiraea prunifolia*)

Camellia (*Camellia japonica*): 'White Empress'

Clematis (*Clematis* species and cultivars): 'Henryi', 'Duchess of Edinburgh'

Deutzia (*Deutzia gracilis*)

Foxglove (*Digitalis purpurea*): 'Alba'

Hydrangea (*Hydrangea macrophylla* and hybrids): 'Mariesii', *H. paniculata* 'Grandiflora'

Lily (*Lilium* species): Asiatic 'Navonna', Oriental 'Casablanca'

Lily-of-the-Valley (*Convallaria majalis*)

Moonflower (*Ipomoea alba*)

Viburnum (*Viburnum* species and hybrids)

Campanula **'Blue Clips'**

Spiky plants, such as obedient plant, add vertical interest to a garden. Since they are often tall, they are best sited at the back of the border.

Plant Forms

The diversity in plant and flower forms is amazing, and a garden that includes as many of them as possible is a full and fascinating place. That is, a garden that uses plants of all sorts "maximizes" its potential and has variety. Usually a plant is small when you receive it in a mail-order shipment or bring it home from the nursery. Assuming it is happy in your yard, it will grow and spread out. So part of understanding plant forms is taking into account mature plant dimensions (expected height and width). This information is provided for every entry in Chapter 5, the Plant Directory, and you will also find it in catalog descriptions and on nursery tags. While it is important, size data should also be viewed only as general guidelines. Your area's weather and your yard's unique conditions will naturally cause some variation. But at least you can get some idea of what to expect.

CAN'T MISS TIP:

SPIKY PLANTS

- **Delphinium** (*Delphinium elatum*)
- **Foxglove** (*Digitalis* species)
- **Gladiolus** (*Gladiolus* × *hybridus*)
- **Hollyhock** (*Alcea rosea*)
- **Larkspur** (*Consolida ambigua*)
- **Mullein** (*Verbascum* species)
- **Obedient Plant** (*Physostegia virginiana*)
- **Pentemon** (*Penstemon* species)
- **Red-Hot Poker** (*Kniphofia uvaria*)

Vertical Plants

Many flowers send up spikes, some or all of their length laden with blossoms. Sometimes flower spikes are single-stemmed, as with red-hot pokers and snapdragons; sometimes they branch to form a candelabra profile, as with certain salvias and mullein. Either form may suit your plans for "vertical interest." Because they often stand tall, flowers in this group are best sited either to the back of a flower border or in the middle of an "island bed" intended to be viewed from all sides. This way, they don't block the view of other, shorter plants. And, hopefully, their companions help hide their "bare knees" from view.

Not all flower spikes stand up as straight and tall as you might wish. They may start to lean over if the flowers are many and heavy or if the plant likes full sun, isn't getting enough, and is straining towards light. If insufficient light is the problem, you might need to relocate the plant. You can also stake it (it's always wise to do this early, partly so the plant can fill in around the stake and hopefully obscure the support from view, and partly because it's not easy to insert a stake and fasten a plant to it late in the game). Or you can grow plants nearby that are substantial and strong enough to help hold up their neighbors.

Low Growers

Low-growing plants are a great help in the garden. They create a carpet of colorful flowers and foliage where there might otherwise be bare ground, which would be an open invitation to weeds.

While some groundcovers and low-growing perennials and annuals, such as perennial sedums and annual lobelia, can be covered with flowers for weeks on end, there will be quiet times. For this reason, you would be wise to select plants whose foliage is attractive, too. You might even consider plants whose leaves are dappled or variegated with cream or white, such as ajuga or lamium, which can provide a bright spot even when they are not in flower.

Mound Formers

The nice thing about plants that naturally grow into a mound is that they combine the best of both worlds. You get height in your garden, but also mass. With this sort of plant, you also get change. Often a mound-forming plant, whether a perennial or ornamental shrub, has a lot of foliage, and may be fairly dense or compact. Stems emerge above the leaves to display the flowers— either high above, or just slightly taller than the foliage. Either way shows off the flowers well while giving your garden multiple layers and plenty of substance or "heft."

Pratia and other low-growing plants can create a colorful carpet of flowers and foliage.

Many flower gardeners use these exclusively; even when the plants are of varying sizes, they weave together to create a filled-in look. Alternatively, you can intersperse mound-forming plants throughout a garden to create continuity—repetition "ties things together," as designers say.

CAN'T MISS TIP:

MOUND FORMERS

- **Bellflower** (*Campanula carpatica*)
- **California Poppy** (*Eschscholzia californica*)
- **Coreopsis** (*Coreopsis* species)
- **Hardy Geranium** (*Geranium* species)
- **Hosta** (*Hosta* hybrids)
- **Lady's Mantle** (*Alchemilla mollis*)
- **Lavender** (*Lavandula angustifolia*)
- **Nasturtium** (*Tropaeolum majus*)
- **Pinks** (*Dianthus* species)
- **Star Cluster** (*Pentas lanceolata*)

Flower Forms

Individual flowers have certain forms, and they are also grouped in certain ways on the stalk. Some clusters are combined in such a way that they appear to be a single flower (such as members of the composite or aster family). Petals can be separate or they can be fused together into a tube. Sometimes the showy parts of a flower aren't petals at all but bracts (modified leaves) or "tepals" (a combination of petals and sepals, such as with daylilies). A few of the more specific terms for flower cluster forms are corymb, raceme, panicle, cyme, umbel, and spike.

But, without getting technical, a few types of *individual* flower forms you will see include the following:

- BELLS, TUBES, OR TRUMPETS: bellflower, flowering tobacco, trumpet vine
- CUPS OR SAUCERS: hardy geranium, nasturtium, poppy
- DOUBLES: baby's breath, peony, rose

A few examples of the different types of flower *clusters* you are likely to find are:

- DAISIES: aster, black-eyed Susan, boltonia, coneflower, coreopsis, Shasta daisy
- SPIRES, SPIKES, AND RACEMES: delphinium, larkspur, Russian sage, salvia, snapdragon
- UMBELS: primrose, Queen Anne's lace, yarrow
- BALLS: bee balm, globe thistle, hydrangea

Many flowering plants, including the many types of hardy geraniums, form attractive clumps, giving the garden mass as well as height.

You may notice, or read about, flowers that are single, semi-double, or double. These occur in a great many types of flower. A single-form flower has one set of petals (a single-form rose has five petals, for example), a semi-double has a few extra petals, and a double form can have numerous petals. Sometimes they are naturally occurring genetic variations and sometimes the unusual form is the work of a plant breeder.

The Tall and Short of It

Including a range of heights is important in a landscape. It makes it look fuller, leads your eye around the garden, and brings excitement. Having tall plants extends garden interest above ground level, bringing valuable dimension to the entire scene.

Height can be temporary, and so you need to decide if that's okay, and where it works best. It can be a bit tricky to place tall plants in your garden, for the simple reason that they don't always come that way or stay that way. Some plants look like bushy mounds until they send up towering bloom stalks. When these flowers finally fade away and you clip off the flowering stems, you lose at least some of the height once again. Examples include Japanese anemone, foxglove, bugbane, queen-of-the-prairie, yarrow, and mullein.

Other tall plants will hold their presence and form quite well for most of the season, even if they are not in prime bloom condition the whole time, and if you leave the flower stalks in place as they go to seed. Examples include delphinium, hollyhock, penstemon, monkshood, and

Flowers come in many forms and sizes, and are grouped on their stems in different ways. A garden that includes a variety of flowers is a more interesting and lively place.

CAN'T MISS TIP:

TAKING SHAPE

If a plant reaches a size and shape that you like, but keeps on growing past that ideal form, you can use your clippers from time to time to keep it tidy and in bounds. Most perennials, annuals, and shrubs respond to trimming during the growing season by becoming more compact. Even low-growing plants benefit from trimming; you'll keep them under control and they'll also flower more densely—a nice plus.

SAVVY BULB SHOPPING

Good-quality bulbs dramatically increase your odds of having a great spring show. Here's what to look for, and remember to start shopping the previous late summer or early fall.

- **Size:** Bigger is, in fact, better. This is because a larger bulb has more food reserves and thus more energy to generate stem, foliage, and flowers. Also, bulbs that start out larger tend to be the ones that return the following spring, with a similar or increased output.

- **Weight:** A healthy bulb is plump and firm because it has moisture reserves; you can easily check this by picking it up and gently squeezing it.

Also, compare it to like ones; a significantly lighter-weight bulb is probably dried out and therefore a dud.

- **Appearance:** Just as you do when shopping for onions in the produce section, you should look closely at a bulb before buying. The outer skin or skins should be intact, not dented or otherwise marred, and show no signs of rot.

If you shop for bulbs by mail (which allows you a great many more interesting choices and is worth doing for that reason alone), obviously you can't look at the merchandise in advance. But inspect the bulbs immediately when your shipment arrives, and if any are substandard, contact the supplier. These companies usually have fair and speedy return policies.

salvia. Of course, if you want height that is more permanent, look to shrubs.

Bloom Times

Achieving a flower garden that always has something in bloom is completely doable, but you have to plan for it. Trial-and-error certainly works, over time anyway, though you can also do some careful research and draw up plans. Most of us end up doing something midway between these approaches. It's also worth trying to get just one season right, even if only in one part of your garden. Success even in one area really buoys your confidence; it also educates you. And then you'll be ready to expand, doing more of the same or trying different ideas in other parts of the yard.

Spring bloomers are not limited to bulbs. Cool-season annuals like Johnny-jump-ups can create an early garden full of flowers.

Spring Bloomers

Beginning the gardening year with lots of splashy color is fun, gratifying—and surprisingly easy. A great many spring bloomers are bulbs, which you plant the preceding fall, so when spring does finally roll around, you can sit back and admire the results of your investment. As you try to decide which bulbs to choose, find out whether they bloom early, mid-season, or late. Using a variety of bulbs in each of these categories assures you a nice long spring of color.

Bulbs do not have a monopoly on spring color, however. Don't forget early-blooming perennials and annuals, such as pansies, hellebores, Virginia bluebells, and bleeding heart. If you wish, these can join the bulbs, and their foliage will remain to help cover over or distract from fading bulb foliage as spring winds down.

And don't forget spring-flowering shrubs. Just one, or a few, can create a spectacle in your yard and fill you with hope and enthusiasm for the garden. Cooler weather also seems to prolong their bloom period. Azaleas and rhododendrons and forsythia are the most common; to make your displays more interesting, seek out improved versions and different colors. Other worthy spring-bloomers are pearlbush, spirea, bridal wreath, broom, California lilac, and mountain laurel.

CAN'T MISS TIP:

FALL CLASSICS

- **Anise Hyssop** (*Agastache foeniculum*)
- **Aster** (*Aster* species)
- **Autumn Crocus** (*Colchicum autumnale*)
- **Boltonia** (*Boltonia asteroides*)
- **Dahlia** (*Dahlia* hybrids)
- **Goldenrod** (*Solidago* species)
- **Japanese Anemone** (*Anemone* × *hybrida*)
- **Mum** (*Chrysanthemum* and *Dendranthema* hybrids)
- **Sedum** (*Sedum* species)
- **Spider Lily** (*Lycoris radiata* and *L. squamigera*)

Summer Bloomers

Summer can be the best and most exciting season in many flower gardens, simply because that's when so many plants bloom, in response to the longer and warmer days. As with spring, summer has its own "sub-seasons," which you would be wise to capitalize on. So as you draw up your wish lists, learn which flowers bloom in early summer, midsummer, and late summer.

Summer can be the best and most exciting season in many flower gardens, simply because that's when so many plants bloom, in response to the longer and warmer days.

SUMMER SUPERSTARS AND FRAGRANCE!

Yes, some plants are capable of blooming with colorful flowers for most or all of the summer months. They tend to be sun-lovers, and they benefit from basic care to give their best (decent soil to grow in, ample water, perhaps some fertilizer, and occasional deadheading). Annuals are very dependable, and you can certainly start there. But some excellent perennials are also up to the job:

- **Bellflower** (*Campanula* species)
- **Blanket Flower** (*Gaillardia* species)
- **Coneflower** (*Echinacea purpurea*)
- **Coreopsis** (*Coreopsis* species)
- **Daylily** (*Hemerocallis* hybrids)
- **Evening Primrose** (*Oenothera* species)
- **Gaura** (*Gaura lindheimeri*)
- **Mallow** (*Malva alcea*)
- **Pincushion Flower** (*Scabiosa columbaria*)
- **Salvia** (*Salvia* species)
- **Shasta Daisy** (*Leucanthemum × superbum*)
- **Valerian** (*Centranthus ruber*)
- **Veronica** (*Veronica* species)
- **Yarrow** (*Achillea* species)

Count on the following plants not only to bring beauty to your summer garden, but delicious fragrance as well. They are mainly sun-lovers, which is good, because warm sunshine releases the volatile oils that hold fragrance in flowers (the oils reside in the petals). Still, "close" days also help keep your garden more fragrant, because humidity slows evaporation.

- **Flowering Tobacco** (*Nicotiana alata*)
- **Gardenia** (*Gardenia augustifolia*)
- **Honeysuckle** (*Lonicera* species)
- **Jasmine** (*Jasminum officinale*)
- **Lavender** (*Lavandula angustifolia*)
- **Oriental Lily** (*Lilium* hybrids)
- **Pinks** (*Dianthus* species)
- **Rose** (*Rosa* hybrids)
- **Stock** (*Matthiola incana*)
- **Summer Phlox** (*Phlox paniculata*)
- **Sweet Pea** (*Lathyrus* species)
- **Sweet Pepperbush** (*Clethra alnifolia*)

Cool fall weather doesn't have to mean the end of the flowering season—many plants are autumn bloomers. The blue of the monkshood flowers and the peachy-gold of the hardy mums add to the show of autumn's warm colors.

Plan to have representatives of all three, and count on some overlapping. Some plants do actually bloom for the entire summer, and these can serve to carry the garden through the season, as shorter bloomers come and go.

Late Summer into Fall

In some gardens, the dog days of August are the beginning of the end of the summer season. Flowers are fading and going to seed, and the color that was such a delight only a few weeks ago is clearly

By including plants with ever-green foliage and winter blooms you can indeed have a full-season garden. Hellebores not only have attractive leaves all year, they have beautiful flowers in winter and early spring.

spent. But it's still pleasant to be outdoors, during the day or for evening relaxing, grilling, or entertaining. So don't let the flower show end too soon! There are many plants that either continue to bloom into autumn, or start flowering toward the end of summer. If you are lucky to live in an area where the foliage of trees and shrubs turns color as the weather cools, setting the late-season landscape ablaze with reds, oranges, yellows and golds, it adds to the show to have colorful flowers as well.

Winter Lull

If you live in a mild climate (Zones 8-11), winter is a relatively quiet time, with some rain to keep things going, but sporadic flowers. Take this opportunity to tidy up the garden and to divide some perennials (some that will take fall or winter division include daylilies, blanket flower, iris, salvia, and many sedums). If you live in a colder climate (Zones 2-7), winter is clearly a time of rest. If snow cover is not good or consistent, mulch your flower beds so your perennials aren't winterkilled.

You can have some winter color and interest if you've left seedheads behind during fall cleanup. Yarrow, sedum, and even purple coneflower may get caps of snow that look rather jaunty. There are also plants that bloom in late winter and early spring. Jump-start the season with hellebores, or some early-blooming bulbs such as crocus or winter aconite. Early-blooming shrubs include witch hazel and wintersweet. And pansies can provide color from fall through late spring.

2

Planting and Care

What Flowers Need to Succeed

gorgeous, multicolored flower displays are not difficult to achieve. All it really takes is a basic understanding of what flowers require, plus a few maintenance tricks to keep the show going as long as possible. To promote attractive, long-lasting flowers, the first step is to create an environment in which they are sure to develop and thrive.

Soil Matters

To generate quality flowers, and plenty of them, a plant needs to get off to a good start. The roots feed the rest of the plant, ultimately nourishing flower development, so let's begin there. The most common cause of poor-looking, sparse-flowering, struggling plants is bad soil. No amount of water and fertilizer is really going to change that. So attend to soil quality before you put a single plant in the ground. If it's not in your plans to dig up and begin an entirely new flower bed, you can at least make sure that individual planting holes are ample and full of good soil.

Most plants do best in soil that is laden with organic matter. Unless you garden on a farm, it's unlikely that your yard's soil is naturally high in organic matter and already wonderfully fertile. Your best bet is to excavate a planting area to a depth that allows for continued root growth: 6 to 12 inches for herbaceous plants and up to several feet for shrubs and trees, depending on the size of the rootball. This is about as far as the roots of most flowering plants will reach. Then mix the native topsoil with organic matter, about half-and-half, if possible (the proportions depend on the quality of your soil as well as how much organic material you can get your hands on); with experience, you will be able to judge how much amending is necessary.

Compost is an easy and inexpensive way to create your own organic soil amendment.

Organic Matter

Organic matter brings important benefits to a garden. It helps the soil retain moisture so you do not have to water as often. It allows essential oxygen in because it loosens the soil and creates air spaces. It provides a favorable environment for beneficial soil organisms, from microscopic ones to earthworms. It allows nutrient-bearing water to enter the soil and drain at a moderate rate so roots can get what they need, yet not rot. Organic matter also helps maintain a near-neutral soil pH, an environment most plants thrive in.

Some examples of different types of organic matter include:

- **COMPOST:** Homemade or store-bought, this material is fabulous for flower gardens. It improves soil structure and also contributes nutrients.
- **ROTTED DECIDUOUS LEAVES:** Fresh leaves are not good—they need to break down first. You can hasten breakdown and prevent matting by chopping or shredding them.
- **DAMPENED PEAT MOSS:** Dry peat moss, alarmingly, remains dry long after it has been dug into your garden, which of course does little good for your soil or plants. So help it absorb and retain moisture by wetting it first.
- **AGED MANURE:** Any vegetarian animal waste is suitable. It should also have composted for a while; fresh manure can burn young roots.
- **OTHER MATERIALS:** Rotted sawdust (from wood that was not chemically treated); weed-free hay or straw, preferably chopped up; composted grass clippings (from a lawn that was not treated with lots of nitrogen fertilizer or weedkiller); worm castings; composted seaweed; alfalfa meal; apple pomace; and mushroom-farm compost—all of these are good sources of organic material.

Good Drainage

Most plants thrive in well-drained soil. This means that the ground is neither overly quick-draining or dry, nor soggy. Water that departs too soon eludes thirsty roots, while standing water eliminates air pockets that supply needed oxygen to roots.

If your soil has so many problems that simply amending it will not be enough, you can build a raised bed of wood, bricks, or stone.

To improve poorly draining soil, such as soil with a high clay content, work when the soil is not wet and slimy and dig in organic matter (and sand, if you like). To improve soil that drains too quickly, such as soil with a high sand content, dig in plenty of organic matter and be prepared to continue adding more every year. A layer of mulch around the plants can also help retain soil moisture.

CAN'T MISS TIP:

MAXIMUM SUNSHINE

Since many flowers love sun, orient your raised bed so it will receive as much light as possible. The long sides should therefore run east to west, so the bed faces south.

Raised Beds

If your yard's soil is just too poor, poorly draining, or otherwise problematic for good flower beds, there is a simple solution: raised beds. These are basically bottomless "boxes" with sides that sit atop the poor soil and hold good, well-drained garden soil. The sides, of course, keep the good soil from washing or eroding away. If deer or rodents are a problem in your area, you can install fencing or line the bottom with chicken wire so digging pests can't get in. Another plus is that a raised bed gives your garden a neat and organized look, even when flowers overflow its edges.

Raised beds can be simple to make out of wood and last many seasons, or they can be permanent structures made of stone or brick. If you start the project in the fall, the soil within will have time to "meld" before spring planting; otherwise, there's no harm in setting up a raised bed in spring. Select a sunny spot where flowers will prosper. Measure a relatively flat area and clear it of all weeds, grass, and debris. Then build the sides and add soil to fill (if the bed is shallow, till up the native soil at the bottom before mixing in amendments and more soil). Or, if you don't want to construct a raised bed, you can achieve much the same affect with a "berm" made by piling soil into a small hill, sloping it down to the level of the rest of the yard.

Light

When you are looking around your yard for a good place to grow flowers, look for sunny spots. Some flowering plants tolerate or even prosper in shade (see pge 57 in Chapter 3 for lists of these), but most of them prefer sunshine and plenty of it. The sunniest spots are generally south or west facing. Trees, buildings, and fences on your property may affect the ideal spots, of course, and the position of the sun in different seasons will regulate the amount of light that reaches any given location. You can observe your

More light is better if your growing season is short. On the other hand, if your summers are long and blazingly hot, your flowers will appreciate a bit of after-noon shade.

yard over an entire year and even take measurements to determine this important information, but if you have been living there for a while, chances are you have a pretty good idea where the sunny areas are.

Why Flowers Need Sun

Flowers need sunlight—or, more accurately, leaves do. Leaves are the primary "engine room" of a plant. The process of photosynthesis requires light to produce the fuel of food for the plant to operate, thrive, and increase in size. Because the lower leaves are always somewhat shaded by the ones above them, long hours of plentiful sunlight with varying angles as the day goes by is important, so that every leaf gets an opportunity to receive light.

How much sun is enough? This certainly depends on which flowers you intend to grow, but generally speaking, a minimum of six hours a day will do. More light is better if your growing season is short. On the other hand, if your summers are long and blazingly hot, your flowers will appreciate a bit of afternoon shade. Too much hot sun dries out petals and fades flower color. (It is the warmth of the sun that inspires flowers to unfurl, by the way, more than the actual light.) Offer a little shelter from the hot midday sun, which can cause even the most sun-loving flowers to flag a bit or fade in color. Either site your flower beds so dappled shadows or light shade fall over them by mid-afternoon or supply some shade with a trellis, taller plants, or even garden furniture.

East vs. West

Sunlight from the east is generally considered cooler, while western sun can be scorching. Many plants prefer a site with morning sun, even until midday, and late afternoon shade. But some plants are able to endure even the hottest conditions. This of course varies by region also. The same plant in the far north can be placed in a sunnier spot than it would be if planted in the south. If you have plants that receive a blast of late afternoon sunlight, be sure to monitor their water needs closely. If you find that a number of plants seem to suffer late in the day, consider installing something that will cast a shadow, such as an arbor, or planting a tree or large shrub in just the right spot. Even companion perennials or annuals planted nearby can cast enough shade to make the difference.

Fertilizer

Even with organically rich, fertile soil, flowering plants can benefit from plant food, or fertilizer. A good, all-purpose, balanced formulation such as 5-10-5 or 5-10-10 contributes to overall plant health and, consequently, good flower production. An extra boost for flowers in particular can come from phosphorus (P), which is the middle number on a container of fertilizer.

The three numbers stand for the relative amounts of the three basic plant growth elements:

- NITROGEN (N), the first number, enhances stem and leaf growth.
- PHOSPHORUS (P), the second number, contributes to flower production, as well as production of fruits and seeds, and root growth.
- POTASSIUM (K), the last number, ensures general vigor. It also helps a plant resist disease.

Even if your soil is rich, flowering plants can benefit from the addition of a balanced, all-purpose fertilizer.

Certain plants demand more or less of these elements, but most garden flowers do not fall into those categories, which is why an all-purpose fertilizer is recommended.

More About Phosphorus

Because phosphorus has been shown to aid bloom production, flower gardeners are naturally interested in providing it for their plants. While a general, all-purpose fertilizer will do the trick, there is a bit more to the story.

It turns out that this particular nutrient is available to plants as phosphate, which bonds to soil and is nearly insoluble. That is, it tends to break down and dissolve so slowly that only a small amount is available to plant roots at any given time. Ideally, you want to get phosphorus into the

There are many kinds of fertilizer, granular and liquid, organic and chemical. Organically based fertilizers tend to be slow release and long lasting, while chemical types have a more immediate affect but do not contribute to long-term soil fertility.

soil, down to the roots (it won't do much good on the soil surface or top few inches). And you will not need to reapply it as often as soluble nutrients.

In addition to traditional mixed fertilizers, you can supply phosphorus with rock phosphate, super phosphate, or bone meal. If you use one of these in your flower beds, be sure to dig it in thoroughly and deeply. And don't let excess granules sit on the soil surface or spill on the driveway, walkways, or patio—phosphorus in runoff is a pollutant.

Enough Food, and Too Much

Plant fertilizer is like aspirin: More is not better! If you over-fertilize, you run the risk of sending nutrients away in runoff (and therefore contributing to water pollution in your region). Also, plants react poorly to overfeeding, usually by generating excessive, lush stem and leaf growth—*at the expense of flowers!* Overfed plants may also be more vulnerable to garden pests and diseases.

So always read and follow the directions on the label. Some fertilizers are best dug into the soil; others are better delivered in dilute form when you water your garden. The label will also tell you how much to use per square foot of garden area, and how often to apply. It's okay to apply half as much, twice as often.

Generally speaking, you should fertilize your flowers starting in spring when growth begins, occasionally throughout the summer months, and then taper off when fall arrives. But watch how your plants respond and adjust your feeding schedule accordingly.

Natural/Organic vs. Chemical/Inorganic

Only you can decide which plant food is convenient and successful for your own garden. Basically a plant doesn't know the difference between one form of an element like nitrogen and another—it's nitrogen in any case. But both natural and chemical types have pros and cons.

So-called natural fertilizers are organically based and tend to be gentler on the soil, and can include beneficial minor nutrients. But they are more slowly released, so their effects are not always dramatic. Examples include homemade or store-bought compost, manure, fish emulsion, cottonseed meal, Milorganite™, blood meal, and bone meal.

Chemical fertilizers tend to be cheap and easy to apply. They come in granules, powders, and concentrated liquids. Dilute them according to the label directions or water them in so they will be activated and so they won't come into direct contact with roots (which can injure or "burn" them). A chemical, quick-release fertilizer can impressively "jump-start" your flowering plants, but don't count on it for long-term soil fertility. The truth is, organic content of any soil is constantly being washed away and lost, especially in cultivated soil. If you use chemical fertilizers exclusively, you'll end up needing to use them on a regular basis.

Water

Everyone knows that flowering plants need water to grow. What you may not know is the best way to deliver water. Here are the basic rules:

- PAMPER NEW PLANTS AND SEEDLINGS WITH LOTS OF WATER. The aim is to encourage the roots to become established, to gain a foothold in their new home.
- WATER DEEPLY. Occasional deep soakings are much better for most plants than frequent shallow waterings. When the water soaks down into the ground, it encourages the roots to follow. Deeper-rooted plants are better able to withstand dry spells (because the top few inches of soil tend to dry out quickly). To check how effective your watering has been, simply dig down with a trowel. You might be surprised to learn that you haven't been providing enough!
- SLOW TRICKLES ARE BETTER THAN HEAVY BLASTS. Water that is delivered slowly has a chance to soak in. If you are delivering water too fast, you'll create runoff, which is not only wasteful, but cheats your plants of something they really need. If runoff still occurs with the slow-trickle method, just stop and start until you are satisfied that enough has soaked in.

Providing adequate water is an essential part of flower gardening. Buds require water to form properly, and flowers need it to stay full and colorful.

One way to conserve water in the soil is to mulch around plants. This also keeps roots cool and minimizes weeds. Types of mulch include bark chips, pine needles, grass clippings, shredded leaves, and weed-free straw.

■ APPLY WATER TO THE ROOTS. Sprinklers and overhead watering are never as effective as water that is delivered straight to the root zone. Evaporation and waste is much less of a concern with on-the-ground watering (as from a soaker hose or a hose set at the base of a plant). Another benefit is avoiding unsightly water spots and rot or other plant diseases caused by water on leaves and flowers.

Why Flowers Need Water

All plant parts benefit from water, but flower buds and consequently flowers love it. This is because buds and flowers consume a lot of water. It plumps them up, fuels their color, and sustains their form.

So water your flowering plants regularly throughout the growing season, but pay special attention when you observe buds forming and swelling. If they suffer from insufficient water during this critical period, the buds may dry out without ever opening or the flowers won't last as long. They'll wilt, drop their petals, or dry up completely. This is because plants naturally give priority to the leaves first and the flowers last (because the leaves are essential to photosynthesis and food production for the entire plant). Plenty of water *before* and *during* flowering is important!

Conserving Water

While it's important to deliver the water needed by your flowering plants, there's no sense in wasting this precious resource. Two excellent ways to make the most of the water you supply are basins and mulch. A basin is simply a bowl made of soil around a plant's base, hopefully encompassing the bulk of the young root zone. When you water, the water collects here and soaks in directly where it is needed. A good rule of thumb is to form the basin's rim at the "drip line," or outer edge of the plant's bulk of foliage and stems.

A mulch layer is important to conserve soil moisture, though it should not be so thick or composed of such a material that it is impenetrable (a layer of plastic is not a good mulch). Nor should it come right up against the crown or main stem of a plant, or rot can occur. Good flower-garden mulches include shredded bark, bark chips, grass clippings,

shredded and rotting leaves, weed-free hay or straw, pine straw, cocoa hulls, compost, and mushroom compost. Landscape fabric will do a fine job, too, though it can be difficult to install after planting is finished, and some types are hard to dig through if you've waited until it is in place to plant. Mulches also keep the weed population down, help reduce erosion, and contribute organic matter to the soil.

PRIME TIME

There is much less evaporation when you water in the early morning or late afternoon. However, morning watering is preferable because the plant can use the water it gets early as it is actively photosynthesizing and growing during the day.

Growing Flowers in Containers

Flowers in hanging baskets, pots, planter boxes, tubs, urns, and so on have special needs compared to their in-the-ground brethren. Or, to put it more accurately, they have the same needs but in a special setting.

- POTS: Clay pots tend to wick moisture away from the soil and roots faster than plastic ones. Consequently plants in these pots may need more regular watering. Alternatively, you can nest a smaller plastic pot inside a larger clay pot.

- SOIL: Heavy garden soil is inadvisable in a container, as it can get waterlogged and the plant roots will rot. (It also makes the container heavy and difficult to move.) It's much better to use a mix without soil, intended for containers.

- DRAINAGE: Don't grow flowering plants in a pot with no drainage holes in the bottom, as rot is a major concern. If you have a decorative pot that lacks drainage holes, try nesting a proper pot inside it, placed atop rocks or bricks to allow water to drain away. Or line the bottom of a non-draining pot with a layer of pebbles or broken crockery, so the plant roots are above any reservoir of collected water.

- SUN: Flowers tend to lean toward the sun and it will be obvious if your potted or hanging plants are not getting enough light. If possible, turn the pot a quarter turn every day or so to assure even, balanced growth and flowering on all sides.

Growing flowers in pots can bring the garden onto your porch or deck, and add a decorative, seasonal element out in the garden.

■ **FERTILIZER:** After a while, potted plants suck all the nutrients out of the soil they're growing in and it becomes mainly an anchoring medium. You can repot in fresh mix, of course, but an easier solution is to fertilize often. (Follow the directions on the label so you don't overfeed: Overfeeding can actually *reduce* flower production.)

■ **WATER:** Pots dry out quickly and roots can soon suffer, with dramatic results showing on the plant above. A stressed plant will jettison buds and flowers first, then leaves. Throughout this slow death, wilting will be obvious. Prevent this from happening with diligent, regular watering. As with garden-grown plants, it's best if you deliver the water right to the roots and avoid splashing the flowers and leaves. But be careful not to over-water either; a plant that continually sits in water isn't receiving the oxygen its roots need.

Deadheading spent flowers interrupts the process of seed production and prompts many plants to continue producing blooms.

A container-grown plant that is too happy ends up outgrowing its home. When this happens, you have three choices. You can try to prevent the inevitable by constant pruning and pinching, which has the desirable side effect of making the plant grow bushier. You can repot the burgeoning plant in a bigger container. Or you can divide it into sections and repot each one in a smaller pot.

Maintaining Your Flowers

Take good care of your flowering plants and they will surely repay your efforts by looking great. Most maintenance consists of basic, commonsense gardening practices, but there are a few additional measures you can take when you are concentrating on flower displays, such as pruning, deadheading, staking, and winter protection.

Pruning and Deadheading

For flowering plants, be careful when you cut them back. Otherwise, you might inadvertently diminish or remove the flower show for this year or the next. (If it's a flowering shrub that produces berries or fruit, you run the risk of reducing the harvest.) This doesn't mean you should never get out your clippers—just wield them at the proper times. On the other hand, deadheading, which means removing spent flowers (usually on annuals and perennials, but also some shrubs), promotes more flowering and should be a regular part of your routine. When you remove flowers just as they are passing their prime, you thwart the natural process of going to seed. The plant is basically fooled into continuing to produce more flowers. (Picking fresh bouquets accomplishes the same thing.)

Pruning is generally intended to control growth or to thin a dense plant. Ironically, when you cut off the end of a twig, although you stop outward growth from that point, the plant redirects energy into the side buds below and the result is a bushier plant. If you truly want to reduce a plant's bulk, you need to cut back entire branches, ideally at ground or trunk level. Shearing and shaping, on the other hand, are minimal "haircuts" meant to improve a plant's appearance during its period of active growth. But any sort of pruning done during the growing season can affect flowering. Here's how to make it work to your advantage, so you can still shape your plants without compromising flower production:

■ PERENNIALS AND ANNUALS: If they bloom in the early part of the summer, you can cut back the stems immediately after flowering ends (removing no more than a third of the plant, as a general rule) and often the plants will respond by generating more growth and sometimes even a less-abundant encore of flowering. This works with delphinium, painted daisy, pinks, and yarrow.

■ FLOWERING SHRUBS: Do not prune all your shrubs indiscriminately or at the same time! There are always exceptions and you should get specific pruning advice from the nursery where you acquire a shrub, though some general rules exist.

Some shrubs produce their flowers on this year's growth, or "new wood," in which case it's only safe to prune, judiciously, in late winter or early spring, when they are emerging from dormancy and the growing season is just starting. These shrubs spend most of spring generating branches and leaves, then burst into bloom in summer. Examples include bluebeard, hydrangea, and sweet pepperbush.

Other shrubs bloom on last year's growth, or "old wood." These are generally the early-spring bloomers. It is safe to prune and shape them immediately after the

Timing is important when it comes to pruning shrubs and perennial vines. When to prune clematis depends on what type it is—a clematis that blooms on new growth should be pruned in early spring, and one that flowers on last year's stems should only be pruned right after it flowers.

To enhance the display of plants like mums and asters, pinch stem tips several times before midsummer to encourage branching and increase flower bud formation.

flowers fade. Any later, and you might be taking off the buds that are developing for next spring's show. Shrubs in this category include azalea and rhododendron, forsythia, lilac, flowering quince, and spicebush.

■ CLEMATIS VINES: It's easy to be confused here. Make sure you ask the nursery exactly what type or species of clematis you are purchasing, and when you should prune it. Alternatively, you can carefully observe whether your flower buds and flowers develop from this year's stems or last year's. The general rules are similar to those for flowering shrubs: Clematis that bloom on new wood can be pruned in spring before growth starts, and clematis that bloom on old wood (the previous season's growth) can be pruned only right after flowering ends.

Staking 101

To help your tall, top-heavy, or naturally floppy plants look their best, staking is an excellent idea. Install supports as early in the season as you can. This way, you won't disturb the growing root system any more than is necessary (plus, because it's entering a new season of growth, it should recover from any accidental damage). Another advantage to early intervention is that usually the plant will grow up and around its support, disguising it from view. Some staking methods include:

■ TWIGS: Salvaged pieces of brush can prop up floppy perennials or shrubs quite well.

■ THIN STAKES: Made of plastic, bamboo, wooden doweling, and so on, these should be plunged into the ground as deeply as possible (and thus you may need some fairly long ones) so they are well anchored.

PINCHING AND DISBUDDING

These are specialized pruning techniques that alter or improve flower production in some plants.

• **Pinching:** Some gardeners remove the growing tips of their plants in late spring or early summer to induce branching, bushiness, and more flowers. Stop pinching by midsummer, so you don't delay the proper blooming time. Plants to pinch include asters and mums.

• **Disbudding:** This involves selectively taking off some of the flower buds so the plant can direct more energy into the remaining ones, resulting in larger flowers. Those who grow flowers for show often employ this technique, and you may want to try it just to get some impressive bouquet blooms. Plants to disbud include dahlias and roses.

FLOWERS THAT SELF-SOW

Some flowers require no effort on your part to display their bounty in your garden. You start out with just a few, and before you know it, you have many. This is because the plants "self-sow," or shed their ripe seeds, which then germinate easily. You can rest assured you'll have many more—either later the same year, if it's still early, or in the following spring or summer.

- **Bachelor's Button** (*Centaurea cyanus*)
- **Calendula** (*Calendula officinalis*)
- **California Poppy** (*Eschscholzia californica*)
- **Columbine** (*Aquilegia* species)
- **Cosmos** (*Cosmos bipinnatus*)
- **Feverfew** (*Chrysanthemum parthenium*)

- **Four O'-Clocks** (*Mirabilis jalapa*)
- **Foxglove** (*Digitalis purpurea*)
- **Larkspur** (*Consolida ambigua*)
- **Lupine** (*Lupinus perennis*)
- **Shirley or Flanders Poppy** (*Papaver rhoes*)
- **Violet** (*Viola* species)

■ STAKES AND STRING: You can tailor the size and rigging to the particular plant. Use soft green twine.

■ METAL PEONY RINGS: These are ideal for peonies, but useful for other perennials as well. Install early and center them over a plant's crown for best results.

Winter Protection Basics

When you invest in perennials, certain flowering vines, and flowering shrubs, you don't want to lose them or see them damaged by a harsh winter. You can avoid all sorts of trouble and disappointment by selecting plants known to be hardy in your zone (if you don't know your USDA Hardiness Zone, a map can be found on the U.S. Department of Agriculture website). If something is too tender for your climate, even your best efforts may not be enough to protect it. To help plants prepare for winter, here are some general maintenance practices to follow.

Although peony rings were originally created for peonies, they are a good way to support other multiple stemmed plants like hardy mums and salvias.

■ REDUCE WATERING. This lets growth slow down so the plant can enter dormancy naturally and at its usual time.

MICROCLIMATES

Even though you live in a particular hardiness zone, there are microclimates within your landscape. Survey your yard for areas that might stay cooler or warmer than the rest of the yard. For example, a protected spot by a south-facing wall will hold heat and can create a place to grow a more tender plant.

■ STOP FERTILIZING. A nutritional boost at this time of year only inspires fresh new growth, which can easily be damaged by fall frosts.

■ APPLY MULCH. Having a layer of mulch on the garden will hold heat and prevent frost heaving. In colder regions, when frost is predicted, cover the flower beds with material that is likely to catch and hold snow, such as evergreen boughs, weed-free straw, or salt-marsh hay. Leave this protective covering in place all winter, removing only in early to mid-spring when the plants start to poke through with new growth.

While the cold of winter is necessary for the natural processes of some plants, it can damage others. Be attentive to your hardiness zone and local weather conditions.

As far as specific types of plants are concerned, the following guidelines should prove helpful.

■ ANNUALS: Just rip them out and toss them on the compost pile. If they're self-sowing types, save some seed as insurance and shake the seedheads around areas where you want the plants to come up next year.

■ TENDER PERENNIALS AND TROPICAL PLANTS: If they aren't already growing in a pot, dig them up and put them in one. Then bring the plants indoors to a cool, nonfreezing place (the garage, a screened-in porch, or a sunroom). Water only sparingly throughout the winter months so they can rest. Resume regular watering and fertilizing in spring only when you see signs of new growth.

■ TENDER BULBS: Dig up the bulbs, corms, and tubers of non-hardy plants, dust them with antifungal powder, and store in a cool, dry place for the winter.

■ PERENNIALS: Cut back spent flowering stalks and foliage, then mulch.

■ VINES AND CLIMBERS: If perennial and hardy in your area, leave it on its support (it might be difficult or impossible to extract it anyway). If it's an annual, a frost will kill it and you can pull it from its support and compost the pieces. If it's a rose, you may be able to lower its canes down to the ground, anchor them, and mulch over them (this applies only to far-north regions; climbing roses in many parts of the country can be left in place for winter).

■ FLOWERING SHRUBS: In late summer or early fall, give them one last good soaking. Don't fertilize, and don't prune. Mulch the root zone if you're concerned about alternating freezing and thawing cycles that might heave a young plant out of the ground. If the shrub is a prized plant and a bit tender in your area, you

If you live in a zone that is too cold for some plants, such as dahlia, you can dig and store them for the winter.

can swathe it in burlap or erect a wire cage around it and stuff that with autumn leaves. For broadleaved evergreens such as rhododendrons and mountain laurels, winter can be a dry season (no moisture can being taken up from the frozen ground), which causes the leaves to curl and dry up; you can combat this problem by spraying the leaves in mid-fall with an anti-dessicant, available at garden centers.

■ FLOWERING TREES: In late summer or early fall, give them one last good soaking. If snowfall is especially heavy and you are worried about branches breaking, tramp outside in your boots after a storm, and shake off the snow or brush it off with a broom.

3

Putting It All Together

everyone has an idea of his or her dream garden. Getting there is definitely a process, but it can be a delightful journey. As you install the plants you like, you will learn more about them and how they grow and flower. Later you might decide to move a few around or replace some. New ideas and new plants enter the picture as time goes by, within one season and certainly from one year to the next. Be flexible, keep your eyes open, and have fun!

Ultimately, a well-balanced garden design is restful and instinctively appealing. A seat-of-the-pants jumble ends up looking more like a random collection of plants than a garden. Remember, the best landscapes are considered an entire unit at the planning stage, rather than a series of small, unrelated projects; this is the main lesson home gardeners can take from the professional landscape designers. Even without all their knowledge or skills, you certainly can and should try to think ahead when starting out.

Whether you're planning a full-scale garden makeover or just adding a small flower bed, it's wise to have a plan. First, assess your landscape, taking note of structures, views, shade and sun patterns during the day, and existing trees and garden areas. Then decide where you want to add or expand beds for flowering plants. The last step is the one you've been leading up to—putting the plants in place. Resist the urge to stock up on beautiful flowering plants until you have developed a plan and know where you want to use them.

Getting a Broad View

There's more to good garden design than selecting and installing the plants. Take an overview of your yard first. The new flower displays need to fit, so the result "looks right" in the existing landscape. To that end, it's best—and simplest—to begin by walking around and assessing. When you look over your yard while thinking about gardening opportunities, you'll find you are viewing it with new eyes, perhaps really seeing it for the first time. Make some decisions now, when it's easier to be critical and to make bigger changes.

Some features are non-negotiable, meaning you will not be changing or removing them. These include, of course, buildings such as your house, garage, carport, or shed. Boundaries with your neighbors, including existing fences, walls, and retaining walls, are also probably going to stay as is. Cast a critical eye on large trees and shrubs. Must you keep them, even if they create large shady areas or shed messy leaves and fruit? Could you remove a few, or hire someone to do so? If you want to or have no choice but to keep large plants, make sure they are healthy and looking good. Prune them, or take out excessive growth or lower branches before you contemplate installing garden areas in the immediate vicinity. Take stock of existing garden areas, even if you intend to completely change what is growing there. Are they big enough? Do you like their "lines" or edging?

Before starting a garden project, take an overview of your existing landscape and determine what works and what doesn't, and what changes would better suit your needs.

Is there enough sun to grow flowers? What do you want to keep and what needs to go? And, of course, where do you want new flower beds?

How Do You View the Garden?

Because your gardening dreams may be ambitious, it's useful to prioritize. Decide where you want to make improvements to existing areas or whether you wish to install a completely new flower garden. The best way to start might be with a location that you see or pass by frequently. These are the questions to ask: What part of the yard needs a pretty garden most? Where do we pass by most often, coming and going? Where do we relax the most, front porch or back patio, or other area? Which window of the house gives the best view of the yard, and exactly what part of the yard (how much of it) do you actually see from that window?

Light Patterns

Because the sun moves across the sky over the course of every day, and sunlight intensity and day length change from summer to winter, the amount of sun and shade varies in a yard. South-facing areas, of course, get the most sunshine. Observe which parts of the yard get morning sun (eastern exposures) and which get afternoon or evening sun (west-facing areas). Structures—most notably buildings but also trees—can block sun or cast long shadows, so don't assume that just because an area faces west that it is receiving full afternoon sun. Observe the light patterns in your yard and

To fully enjoy your landscape, first discover how you view the garden, from both inside and outside the house.

Consider how you plan to use your garden space. If you frequently spend time on your porch, deck, or patio, you might want to concentrate your gardening efforts in the area surrounding it, and include a few potted plants.

become familiar with them. Places with maximum sunshine are important to identify, because many flowering plants need as much light as they can get to thrive. Your best starting point is to figure out where the sunniest spots are, and then plan flower beds accordingly.

Using the Garden

Here's another place for honesty—how do you plan to use the garden? Flower gardening should be a pleasure for you, and the amount of effort you put into it should be truly tailored to your lifestyle.

■ RELAXING: If lounging in the hammock or hanging out on the deck or front porch is your idea of the best use of your yard, don't plan a big, ambitious garden. Instead, install low-maintenance flower beds, full of plants that don't require much fussing over.

■ ENTERTAINING: If you like to have people over for outdoor meals or parties, plan your garden accordingly. Place the most impressive looking or longest blooming (or evening blooming) flowers in the foreground. Use potted plants so you can move the ones that are looking their best into full view before the guests arrive. Grow "cutting garden" flowers so you can pick bouquets to decorate for the events.

■ PUTTERING: If you truly enjoy poking around the yard, clipping something here, enjoying the fragrance of something there, tugging out weeds as you go, then grow a variety of flowers, even those requiring some maintenance, knowing that you will be attentive to them.

CAN'T MISS TIP:

TAKE A SEAT

If you know you will be viewing the garden from a particular spot inside or outside the house, spend time looking from that viewpoint and evaluating. If you expect to be seated, then actually sit down and then take stock of the scene. You want to enjoy the garden from the true vantage points you will have as you go about your daily routine.

■ PROJECT-ORIENTED GARDENING: If you acknowledge that you are a hardcore gardener, and have the desire, time, and energy to constantly tinker in your yard, or if you just love gardens and plan to hire landscape help, you can embark on a more extensive plan. Plant many flowering plants, find and place enhancing items (from a trellis to a garden pond to a gazebo), and have fun with it all.

■ JUST SOMETHING PRETTY: If all you want is a nice flower bed to see from the dining room window, or you want your yard to look good to your family and neighbors without a lot of maintenance, then keep it simple. Add a few plantings in key locations, using shrubs and perennials that bloom for a long time or are attractive when not in flower, and pockets of colorful annuals and bulbs.

Creating Garden Areas

Once you know where you want your flower displays, it's time to install them. You can do this in the fall, when you are less distracted by all the growing and blooming plants around you and when you may even have more time. Or you can start in the spring, when you are full of energy and enthusiasm and the garden centers are overflowing with intriguing plants. Another approach is to take the project in stages: installing bulbs, a portion of the perennials, some of the woody plants, and cool-weather annuals such as pansies in the fall; and planting other perennials and woody plants, and

GETTING YOUR BEARINGS

Here are two design principles that will help when getting started with your garden design.

- **Big Things First:** What would best surround or set off your displays—lawn, a patio or deck, a screen of shrubs and trees? Make sure that these features are the way you like them (that they're big enough, where you want them, and of the shape you want), and then add your flower garden or gardens.

- **Compatible Lines:** Help your flower garden look natural and comfortable by taking your cue from the "lay of the land." You shouldn't force a formal, straight-lined flower bed if your yard has hills and dales. On the other hand, don't get too fancy with wavy edges to beds or borders—these are extra work to maintain!

The basic idea is to think about your entire yard and all its elements—to step back and "think big"— as you add new or update older flower-garden areas.

warm-weather annuals in the spring. This can divide the labor between two seasons if you are tackling a large project.

Commonsense Layout

Some sense of proportion between your home, outbuildings such as a shed or garage, and the gardens you install is important. The scene is more pleasing to the eye if you keep things in scale with one another. For instance, a big house does best with higher hedges, wider paths, taller trees or groupings of trees, and larger flower beds. Similarly, a smaller house is enhanced by a series of smaller flower beds, narrower walkways, lower shrubs and hedges, and smaller trees.

Draw a rough map of your property, sketching existing elements and the beds you are planning. Or lay a hose, rope, or outdoor electrical cords along the bed lines you anticipate. Note that longer beds look better if they are also wide; extremely narrow flower beds can look thin and cramped. But keep in mind that overly wide ones look chunky and are difficult to wade into for maintenance.

Within individual flower beds, you can adapt the same tactics by drawing a layout, or placing pots or flats of plants in the bed while you stand back and think about whether they look right. These simple techniques will help you decide issues of symmetry, discover whether one plant might block another from view, check if color combinations will work, and determine whether you need more or fewer plants. Keep in mind the mature sizes of plants, and not just how they look in their containers at the moment, so you won't have to move plants later to allow them more space. You can also stage a "dress rehearsal" using empty pots or trays to get a sense of placement and quantities before you go shopping for plants.

Adding to Existing Gardens

Once you get into flower gardening, you may discover that you need more space to try new plants and new ideas, or to expand the areas you already have. When you have existing garden areas but intend to improve or expand them, take stock of what is there, create a new plan, and stick to it as much as possible (though all plans will likely go through changes as you progress). It's

When planning a flower bed, keep the width and length in pleasing proportions, and in scale with your house and such elements as fences, paths, arbors, or a garden shed.

a good idea to establish the new boundaries before you deal with the interior of the planting bed. Dig a shallow trench around the perimeter and remove weeds and sod. You can even go ahead and install edging materials.

The process of expanding a garden may involve some or all of the following: removing, moving, or pruning existing plants; tearing up turf or digging out weeds; improving the soil in certain spots; and creating planting holes for new plants. As you work, keep your eyes on the prize: A bigger, better garden will be your payoff.

Creating a New Garden

If you are starting from scratch, this is a wonderful opportunity to achieve just the effect you want—and the best time to make the soil perfect for growing healthy, lush plants. As with expanding an existing bed, create a boundary with a pleasing line, and remove all plants that are in the way (lawn or weeds). Turn the soil and amend it with organic material. Then lay out the plants, starting with the "bones"—small trees and shrubs—then progressing with perennials, bulbs, and annuals.

The design of a brand-new flower garden should take into account the following considerations:

- Is there enough sunshine? (If not, figure out if you can let more in, either by moving or pruning a big plant, or removing a structure.)
- Is the soil decent? (If not, work to amend it or install raised beds.)
- Does the size suit the site?
- How will you water it? (Now is the time to install an in-ground irrigation system, if you want one. Otherwise, a water source should be nearby.)

Choosing Plants

This is probably everybody's favorite part! Garden space is ready and waiting. It's time to "furnish" it! As you select plants for your flower beds, aim for a varied show. Think in terms of combinations or scenes, colors you like, and forms and textures that are compatible. There is plenty to consider—but don't feel daunted. You'll learn as you go along, and soon you'll be able to make informed decisions and have a successful garden that suits your wants and needs.

Bloom Times

One of the first things to find out about a flower that catches your fancy is when it blooms—and how long the flowering lasts. This information is provided for every plant in Chapter 5 and is listed on plant tags and in catalog descriptions. You can concentrate on one season, or be ambitious and plan for color from earliest spring well into fall. The best way to organize your thoughts and plans is to make a "wish list" and be sure each season is well represented. Of course, results in your own garden may vary and some flowers will bloom a long time, or span several seasons, but a balanced list will get your displays off to a good start.

Height and Width

It bears repeating and remembering that plants do grow. Those tiny seedlings or potted plants set out in spring may sprawl far and wide by late summer or in ensuing years. Know the mature sizes of plants so you will have no surprises. It's also important to allow plants ample room for other reasons: Crowded plants may be stunted or distorted, flower less prolifically, and suffer from diseases that strike when air circulation is poor. And of course a big plant placed in front of a smaller one will steal the spotlight and spoil the picture you had hoped to create. So do this bit of homework first so you can place plants wisely.

Basic Color Principles

A little acquaintance with certain design principles can really help when selecting and placing plants. Color theories explain why some hues contrast and others fit together. Understand these, and you will have the ability to create pleasing garden scenes. Here is a quick overview that will get you started on making appealing, successful flower combinations.

■ PRIMARY PARTNERS: Bold blue, red, and yellow used together are the starting point for many painters as well as garden colorists. These colors share the same "strength" and therefore always look grand together.

■ OPPOSITES ATTRACT: On a standard artist's color wheel, hues that are directly across from one another are considered complementary. Opposites tend to look great together, both because they

Complementary colors (which are opposite each other on the color wheel) are considered good companions. Here yellow lady's mantle is a dynamic partner for purple salvia.

WINNING PRIMARIES

You can't go wrong when you make a flower display devoted to bright, bold blue, red, and yellow. The result is always substantial and splashy. Here are a few favorites—mix and match to come up with your own combinations.

- **Yellow Flowers:** Coreopsis, Roses, Yarrow, Lilies

- **Blue Flowers:** Veronica, Delphinium, Hardy Geranium, Bellflower, Globe Thistle

- **Red Flowers:** Salvia, Clematis, Zinnia, Bee Balm, Crocosmia

are of similar intensities and because there is striking contrast: for example, purple with yellow, or blue with orange.

■ COMPATIBILITY: Colors that fall between primary colors (called secondary colors) tend to be harmonious companions. Examples are yellow-orange with violet-blue, or red-orange with blue-green. Also, secondary colors look good with their primary neighbors, such as yellow-orange-red and pink-purple-blue.

■ MONOCHROMATIC DISPLAYS: Different shades of a color work well when grouped in a garden display. For example, shades of light and dark yellow, or light and dark purple. Or all white, a favorite approach for those who enjoy their garden mainly in the evening hours when drifts of white flowers really glow.

Hot and Cool Colors

Flower colors can be used to lead the eye, add depth and dimension, and create moods:

■ Cooler colors and pastels have a calming effect and seem to recede.

■ Blues and purples add dimension and suggest more depth, so are good for small gardens.

■ Warmer colors advance. As they add excitement, they can also fool the eye into thinking that they are closer than they are.

If you want to draw attention to some part of the garden, or want a distant location to seem closer, use a bright color. If you have a small garden

The popularity of pastel colors in the garden is partly due to the sense of serenity they impart. They are also easy to use in combinations, with each other and with brighter hues.

and the plants are close to the visitor, use cool colors and purple to give the garden depth. To put these "tricks" to work in your garden, experiment to see what works. You may have to add additional plants to get the full benefit of the colors you want to employ.

Hot colors are the brightest, boldest ones in the spectrum, namely red, orange, and bright yellow. Flowers in this range add welcome cheer, intensity, and excitement. There are also electric shades of fuchsia pink and lime green that have the same effect. Grow a block of one color or combinations and relish how they add punch to your garden. Or use a hot colored flower as an accent plant. If you find your hot-colored flowers are a bit too strident, bright, or aggressive in their demand for the garden spotlight, you can tone them down a bit. An effective way to do this is to pair the bright color with a softer version of the same hue—for instance, a bright yellow bloomer can be joined by a calmer pastel yellow.

For a sense of cool beauty and soothing harmony, the softer-hued flowers carry the day. The pastels—which include pink, softer shades of purple and

Foliage can add color, as well as substance, to the garden— the striking leaves of purple alumroot and gray lamb's ear enhance the delicate form and color of blue bellflower.

EXTRA COLOR FROM LEAVES

If your garden needs an extra jolt of color somewhere, but you want that color to be stable and long lasting, consider tucking in some plants with purple or burgundy foliage, or splashy, striped, or variegated leaves. Here are some dependable favorites:

- **Barberry** (*Berberis thunbergii*): 'Atropurpurea', 'Golden Ring', 'Rose Glow'
- **Bugleweed** (*Ajuga reptans*): 'Atropurpurea', 'Burgundy Glow'
- **Caladium** (*Caladium bicolor*)
- **Canna** (*Canna × generalis*): 'Red King Humbert', 'Striped Beauty'
- **Coralbells** (*Heuchera* species and hybrids): 'Palace Purple', 'Montrose Ruby'

- **Coleus** (*Coleus* hybrids)
- **Elephant's Ear** (*Alocasia macrorrhiza*): 'Hilo Beauty', 'Black Magic'
- **Lungwort** (*Pulmonaria* species and cultivars)
- **Smokebush** (*Cotinus coggygria*): 'Royal Purple', 'Velvet Cloak'
- **Sweet Potato Vine** (*Ipomoea batatas*): 'Blackie'
- **Tricolor Sage** (*Salvia officinalis* 'Tricolor')

Gray-leaved plants are particularly well suited for supplying relief for the eye in colorful flower gardens. They highlight brighter colors, yet flatter pastels beautifully. Some tried-and-true favorites for this important job are dusty miller (*Senecio cineraria*), lamb's ears (*Stachys byzantina*), and artemisia (*Artemisia* species and cultivars).

blue, and lighter shades of yellow, cream, and white—bring serenity to a garden, in simple displays as well as in more extensive groupings. Vary plant habits, textures, and heights so the display is as interesting as it is pretty.

Texture and Placement

When laying out a garden bed, mixing and matching applies not only to flower color, but to the sizes and forms of the plants you choose. The overall look of a plant is often referred to as its "texture" (using words like "bold," "coarse," or "delicate"). Savvy use of texture helps to make a display beautiful and interesting. But how do you avoid creating an overly busy or monotonous look? Within the context of the entire garden, provide a combination with both variety and continuity. If an area is narrow or small, use a simple combination of only a few textures. Trying to stuff too many plants into a limited space ends up looking like a hodge-podge. Aim instead for artful simplicity. In a large bed, combine and group plants to lead the eye through the garden, creating interest without being overwhelming.

■ GROUPING: Instead of only planting one of each kind of plant, use several for more impact. Groups of three or five are a good place to start. Odd numbers look more natural, probably because even numbers look a bit *too* symmetrical. If you plant a large group, punctuate the scene with an occasional contrasting color or form.

COMBINING FLOWER FORMS

The best approach to making pleasing and interesting combinations of different flower forms is to be sure to include both spiky types and rounded ones.

Good Spiky Flowers:
- **Delphinium** (*Delphinium elatum*)
- **Foxglove** (*Digitalis purpurea*)
- **Mullein** (*Verbascum* species)
- **Penstemon** (*Penstemon* species)
- **Red-Hot Poker** (*Kniphofia uvaria*)
- **Salvia** (*Salvia* species and hybrids)
- **Veronica** (*Veronica* species)

Good Round Flowers:
- **Allium** (*Allium* species)
- **Coreopsis** (*Coreopsis* species)
- **Hardy Geranium** (*Geranium* species)
- **Petunia** (*Petunia* × *hybrida*)
- **Pincushion Flower** (*Scabiosa columbaria*)
- **Shasta Daisy** (*Leucanthemum* × *superbum*)
- **Zinnia** (*Zinnia elegans*)

■ REPETITION: Intersperse individuals of the same plant, or plants with the same general look, throughout the bed or border at intervals. Try repeating the same color here and there. Or use different forms with the same coloration (flower *or* leaf). All of these schemes have the effect of unifying the entire scene.

■ VARIETY: It's easy to fill a bed with too many plants having similar textures, especially medium to fine, because so many plants have small leaves and flowers. Include both bold and delicate textures. Bold textures can dominate the garden if they are too prominent in the foreground and finer ones can nearly disappear if they are too far in the background, so placement is important also. Having variety allows you to distinguish individual plants, and enjoy them more.

Plant Roles

Different types of flowers can play different roles in your yard. Certain plants are good structure-setters for a flower garden, or you may be seeking a terrific "focal point" plant around which to build a garden scene. Certain flowers are valuable because they bloom over a long period, and some specialize in a certain season or look their best only during a limited period. Some plants even bridge seasons. Others are useful for filling gaps in the garden, so there is always color. Whatever you need, there are myriad choices.

Good Bones

Tending to the largest elements first is the operating rule in and around a flower garden. Look to flowering shrubs (and small flowering trees), including rosebushes, to provide structure—the "bones" of the garden. Such larger plants provide a stabilizing or anchoring influence, giving the display permanence as less substantial bulbs, annuals, and perennials cycle in and out of bloom. Because of their larger size, carefully consider placement of such plants within a flower garden.

■ BACKDROPS: By placing shrubs and small trees at the back of the border, smaller plants are not blocked

Shrubs, such as roses, can give a garden long-term substance, as other plants go in and out of bloom.

Flowering plants, particularly vines such as coral honeysuckle, can be used to cover and enhance structures.

from view, and the foliage creates a background against which colorful flowers show up better.

■ WITHIN BEDS: Placing shrubs in the middle of beds can give definition (and something of interest in winter). Just don't allow them to overwhelm neighboring plants: Give woody plants ample room to achieve their mature sizes, or keep the plants well pruned so they stay in bounds.

Structure for your yard can also come in the form of hedges and screens, or "living fences." Rather than a real fence or wall, you may prefer that living plants define your garden's boundaries. This can help your garden look more natural, create a sense of privacy, and keep out intruders. And while they can be a barrier against wind, too much hot sun, and street noise, they also allow air circulation. These plants can also bring beauty, including flowers and berries. Lilacs, viburnums, forsythia, butterfly bush, beautyberry, hydrangea, and California lilac are all pretty choices. But these are only suitable if you don't want a formal or clipped look to the boundary, because constant or significant pruning will remove flower buds and alter the plant's natural profile.

CLIMBING FLOWERS

Sometimes the "bones" of your garden are man-made structures such as fences and trellises, but to make the scene look more natural and much prettier, you can cover them with colorful flowers and foliage. Here are a handful of suitable choices. For more, consult the Chapter 5 section on vines and climbers, or peruse the choices at your local nursery.

- **Black-Eyed Susan Vine** (*Thunbergia alata*)
- **Climbing Nasturtium** (*Tropaeolum majus*)
- **Climbing Rose** (*Rosa* hybrids)
- **Honeysuckle** (*Lonicera sempervirens*)
- **Morning Glory** (*Ipomoea tricolor*)
- **Scarlet Runner Bean** (*Phaseolus coccineus*)
- **Sweet Autumn Clematis** (*Clematis paniculata*)

Another way to landscape a fence is to plant tall flowers all around it, on both sides. This creates a living boundary, giving your garden a lush, casual look. Foxgloves, cleome, hollyhocks, and lilies of various kinds are all good choices. As with the climbers, you want to be careful not to make a planting hole right under or too close to the fence, otherwise the plants could have trouble standing up or spreading out naturally.

You might enjoy mixing various shrubs together within a row, screen, or hedge. This makes a more interesting display, and allows you to savor various types of shrubs. But because it is so variable, of course a mixed shrub border has a more informal look. The best formal hedges are plants that grow thickly and respond well to shaping and shearing, such as yew, laurel, barberry, boxwood, and holly.

Focal-Point Plants

Nothing else commands attention, anchors a garden scene, and delights garden visitors quite like a well-chosen "focal-point" plant. It may be grown in the ground, in a pot, or even a pot on a pedestal. It can be any plant you feel is dramatic, because of size, color, or texture. And any number of plants can be used as focal points depending on what is planted around it—a fine-textured plant among bolder companions, a bold plant among delicate ones, a dark or bright color among pastels or vice versa. Often a focal-point plant is bigger than those around it, so all eyes naturally turn to it. It therefore needs to have sufficient room, so take into account its projected mature size—on all sides—when you choose and site it.

A plant can also serve as a focal point if it has a standout color—lighter, darker, or more vivid than its surroundings. A bright red flower such as hibiscus immediately draws the eye. White flowers (even a patch of daisies) can be a beacon in the garden. And dark purple flowers and foliage surrounded by lighter colors can add depth, such as dark-leaved canna planted near lime-green sweet potato vine or silvery maiden grass. The bold texture of the canna also makes it stand out if it's near plants with smaller leaves and flowers.

A focal-point plant may benefit from being displayed in a container. You can use an ordinary clay pot, or a big decorative urn, barrel, or otherwise impressive or imposing vessel. Make sure both the pot and its contents look good from all viewing angles. Even the most ordinary plant, when paired imaginatively with a good container, can be vaulted into garden stardom.

Plants for the Long Haul

Two types of plants are worth investing in if you wish for longevity— plants that bloom over a long period, and plants that live a long time.

REAL STANDOUTS!

Here is a list of plants that have proven to be good focal-point plants. Remember to seek out something that will look grand when viewed from different angles. Having dramatic foliage also makes a plant really stand out.

- **Angel's Trumpet** (*Brugmansia arborea*)
- **Bear's Breeches** (*Acanthus mollis*)
- **Canna** (*Canna × generalis*)
- **Foxglove** (*Digitalis purpurea*)
- **Hibiscus** (*Hibiscus* species)
- **Red-Hot Poker** (*Kniphofia uvaria*)
- **Rose** (tree-form *Rosa* hybrids)

A plant with striking color and form can be a focal point in the garden.

LONG-HAUL FAVORITES

Rely on these plants to produce flowers for most of the growing season.

- **Angelonia** (Angelonia angustifolia)
- **Black-Eyed Susan** (Rudbeckia species)
- **Catmint** (Nepeta × faassenii)
- **Coneflower** (Echinacea purpurea)
- **Daylilies** (repeat-blooming Hemerocallis cultivars)
- **Impatiens** (Impatiens walleriana)
- **Lantana** (Lantana species)
- **Petunia** (Petunia × hybrida, especially the Wave Series)
- **Rose** (Rosa varieties, especially modern ones)
- **Salvia** (Salvia species, perennial and annual)
- **Summer Phlox** (Phlox paniculata)
- **Zinnia** (Zinnia elegans and Z. linearis)

Native plants, such as mistflower, are adapted to local conditions, making them durable (as well as beautiful) additions to the garden. Discover the garden-worthy plants native to your region and include them in your landscape.

To get a superior performance, the plants need to be growing where they're happy, and should be well maintained (with regular watering, fertilizing, and deadheading as needed). While plenty of plants have handsome foliage over a long period, those with long-lasting flowers most endear themselves to gardeners who relish color in their garden.

■ LONG-BLOOMERS: Plants that spend many long weeks in bloom keep your garden colorful and save you work. This is why annuals, in particular, continue to be so popular and valuable. But many perennials and some shrubs, such as roses, can bloom for much of the season.

■ LONG-LIVED PLANTS: Some plants—roses, peonies, daylilies, hellebores, and woodland wildflowers—seem to outlast generations as they bloom year after year. The key is often hardiness, or the ability to survive the winters in your area. So always make a point of checking hardiness when looking for plants that you want to last many years in your garden.

Quick Color

At times you may simply want a plant that delivers its flowers abundantly and quickly. Maybe you've planned an important event in your garden, such as a party or wedding, and want part of your yard to look good quickly. Or maybe you've planted slow-growing perennials, biennials, or shrubs that need a growing season to get going, and you want something to decorate the area temporarily. Whatever the reason, help is on the way. There are three good ways to get fast color:

■ Tuck in some annuals.

■ Get larger, more mature perennials or flowering shrubs (which will cost more, of course, but may be worth it!).

■ Place potted blooming plants strategically where color is most needed.

A YEAR OF FLOWERS

Flowers bloom in practically every season, at least in mild climates. However, the majority of bloomers peak in spring and summer, so these are the times of the year with the greatest opportunities for garden color. You'll want to plan for each season to get the most out of your garden. The easiest way to do this is to make wish lists organized by bloom time (this information is listed for every plant in Chapter 5, plus you'll find it on plant tags, in reference books, and in plant catalogs; when in doubt, ask a knowledgeable gardener). Here's a quick overview to point you in the right direction, if you're just starting out.

The ultimate garden is one that changes with every season, providing a continuing parade of color and interest, but that takes careful planning. You want plants that not only bloom reliably and handsomely but are also good citizens in a mixed flower bed. Making a shopping list is a starting point, but beyond that, it takes trial and error (what performed well? what was crowded?) to refine the show from one year to the next. Here are some simple plant combinations to help get your flower-garden plans started.

Early:

Candytuft (*Iberis sempervirens*)
Creeping Phlox (*Phlox subulata*)
Daffodil (*Narcissus* species and hybrids)
Grape Hyacinth (*Muscari* species)
Hellebore (*Helleborus orientalis*)
Tulip (*Tulipa* species and hybrids)

Middle:

Black-Eyed Susan (*Rudbeckia* species)
Coneflower (*Echinacea purpurea*)
Lilies (*Lilium* species and hybrids)
Penstemon (*Penstemon* species)
Pincushion Flower (*Scabiosa columbaria*)
Spike Speedwell (*Veronica spicata*)

Late:

Aster (*Aster* species)
Boltonia (*Boltonia asteroides*)
Goldenrod (*Solidago* species)
Mums (*Chrysanthemum* and *Dendranthema*)
Perennial Sunflowers (*Helianthus angustifolius* and others)
Sedum (*Sedum* 'Autumn Joy')

Make sure the planting places are ready, then visit garden centers and select plants looking their best. Buy annuals in smaller pots earlier, allowing them time to get established in the garden or container and start filling in. Perennials and shrubs can be planted closer to the event, and select plants just starting to bud; plants in full bloom might be nearly finished by the time of the party.

Garden Rooms

A garden can be an outdoor room, with plants in the roles of floors, walls, and ceilings. While the lawn is a common "floor" for a garden space, floor plants also include groundcovers, and any low-growing perennial, annual, or shrub. While the "walls" of a garden room can be structures like walls or fences, flowering vines, shrubs, and tall perennials (and even tall annuals like sunflowers) can also create a backdrop and serve as a wall. A garden "ceiling" can be an arbor draped with wisteria or a climbing rose, or the spreading branches of trees.

CAN'T MISS TIP:

GROW NATIVE!

Particularly durable are native plants, because they are already well adapted to your growing conditions and predisposed to perform long and well. To find good native plants for your area, give a local landscaper a call, visit your nearest botanical garden to see ones on display, or shop at a local nursery that advertises that it sells natives.

COLOR BOOSTERS

Here are some tried-and-true methods for getting maximum color from flowers.

- **Fertilize:** Plant food, especially when applied at the beginning of the growing season when plants are poised to launch, makes a big difference. Just remember that more is not better; follow the dosage and delivery information on the fertilizer label.

- **Intermix colorful foliage:** Some plants, coleus for instance, come in a splendid range of colors and color combinations these days; mix a few of these with your slower-blooming flowers to better show off the blooms. Select flowering plants that also have variegated foliage. Lots of perennials and annuals and certain shrubs come in varieties that have leaves splashed with white, yellow, gold, or even red or pink. These keep a display interesting.

- **Deadhead:** Remove spent flowers to keep blooms coming on through the season.

- **Contrast and complement:** Plant something with a complementary or strongly contrasting color nearby—yellow with purple, blue with orange, red with white.

CAN'T MISS TIP:

"FLOOR" PLANTS

For Sun
- **Candytuft** (*Iberis sempervirens*)
- **Lilyturf** (*Liriope muscari*)
- **Pinks** (*Dianthus* species)
- **Sedum** (*Sedum* species)
- **Thrift** (*Armeria maritima*)
- **Thyme** (*Thymus* species)

For Shade
- **Ajuga** (*Ajuga reptans*)
- **Lamium** (*Lamium maculatum*)
- **Lily-of-the-Valley** (*Convallaria majalis*)
- **Periwinkle** (*Vinca minor*)
- **Phlox** (*Phlox stolonifera*)
- **Sweet Woodruff** (*Galium odoratum*)

Garden rooms can create a sense of enclosure, divide a large landscape into more intimate spaces, and make a small landscape seem larger by hiding some of the garden from view as the visitor moves through the rooms. Within the boundaries of these outdoor spaces you can place annuals, perennials, shrubs, bulbs, and small trees, almost like arranging furniture.

Types of Gardens

There are many different types, themes, and moods of gardens. In general the style of a garden can be formal, with crisp edges, symmetry, and a limited plant palette, or informal, with less restrictive boundaries, asymmetry, and a wider variety of plants. But there are many variations in between. Selecting a style can be based on the architecture of your house, the lay of the land, or your personal taste. The type of garden also depends on the amount of sunshine the area receives; sunny gardens and shady ones each have their own unique charm.

Sunny Gardens

Because so many flowering plants love sunshine, a naturally sunny yard is a great boon—allowing a wonderfully broad range of plant choices. Many sun plants bloom in high summer, but you'll want to capitalize on the array of possibilities by also choosing plants that bloom in spring and fall. This way, you'll have continual color over your entire growing season—a sight to be proud of!

Avoid, however, the pitfall of planting too many similar, summer-blooming flowers. For example, many members of the Aster family, such as black-eyed Susan, coneflower, coreopsis, and Shasta daisy are popular and widely available, but they all have daisy-like flower forms. Similarly, there are numerous wonderful salvias, all with spiky flower heads. An overabundance of these will mass together before your eyes and the result is a less interesting garden than you might have hoped for. You should certainly grow these wonderful flowers—just intersperse them with other types of plants.

Meadow Gardens

A meadow garden is the ultimate informal, sunny landscape. Though it seems carefree, it can take some effort to achieve a "natural look." Of course, memories of these efforts vanish when the finished project comes alive with color! And an established meadow can be a low-maintenance alternative to lawns and more intensive garden areas. Be aware that a pretty meadow-garden display can change, since there is no sure way to predict which plants will dominate from one year to the next. But variety and spontaneity are one of the reasons meadow gardens are so enjoyable.

A meadow should have a combination of native grasses (such as little bluestem, big bluestem, broomsedge, and switch grass) and "forbs"

With its foot-long clusters of lavender flowers, wisteria is a popular "ceiling" plant. Be sure to provide it with a sturdy, durable support since it can be a massive and long-lived vine.

RELIEF IN THE SHADE

Ironically, you might need to offer your sunny garden a bit of shade. Continuous sun all day long can stress some plants; sufficient water will help them cope, but a little shade can provide a break. Strong sunlight tends to bleach out colorful flowers and cause white or pastel ones to flag, and also makes all hues less durable and long lasting. Particularly if your sunny garden faces full-on south, a little afternoon shade, at least, could be welcome. If your house or trees don't offer any, you can add shade with taller plants or a structure like a gazebo or arbor.

(meaning other herbaceous flowering plants). Many "meadow seed mixes" consist of annual wildflowers and perennial grasses. This is fine, but depending on the species, the grasses may take over in the second season and the annuals may self-sow with varying success. Meanwhile, biennials and slow-growing perennials may be coming into their own. So you can let nature take its course, or start over and replenish with a fresh mix every spring. You can also include young plants to create a more stable combination of annuals, perennials, and grasses. Contact local experts to learn more about meadow-type plants that are native to your area, as they are the most likely to succeed in your climate and soil. Check city ordinances before installing a meadow (especially in the front yard) since some areas place restrictions on such wild plantings.

A meadow garden can be a magical place, and a great habitat for butterflies, birds, and other wildlife.

Shady Gardens

To look at many gardening magazines and books, it seems like a successful flower garden is by definition sunny. But what if you have shade? Good news—many flowering plants actually thrive in the shade. Some take advantage of springtime's extra light (when deciduous trees overhead are not yet fully leafed out), while others simply perform better in the shade and offer

MEADOW MAGIC

A few good meadow plants include:

- **Bachelor's Buttons** (Centaurea cyanus)
- **Bee Balm** (Monarda didyma)
- **Black-Eyed Susan** (Rudbeckia species)
- **Blanket Flower** (Gaillardia species)
- **Blazing Star** (Liatris species)
- **Bluestar** (Amsonia species)
- **Boltonia** (Boltonia asteroides)
- **Butterfly Weed** (Asclepias tuberosa)
- **Coreopsis** (Coreopsis species)

- **Downy Phlox** (Phlox pilosa)
- **False Blue Indigo** (Baptisia australis)
- **Goldenrod** (Solidago species)
- **Purple Coneflower** (Echinacea purpurea)
- **Queen Anne's Lace** (Daucus carota)
- **Sunflower** (Helianthus species)
- **Wild Bergamot** (Monarda fistulosa)
- **Yarrow** (Achillea species)

SHADY FLOWER FAVORITES

Light-colored flowers show up best, glowing in the shadows and adding a sense of dimension to previously dull, dim areas.

Tolerant of Dry Shade:
- **Columbine** (Aquilegia species)
- **Daphne** (Daphne odorata)
- **Epimedium** (Epimedium species)
- **Hardy Geranium** (Geranium species)
- **Hellebore** (Helleborus orientalis)
- **Periwinkle** (Vinca minor)
- **Solomon's Seal** (Polygonatum species)

Prosper in Damp Shade:
- **Astilbe** (Astilbe × arendsii)
- **Bleeding Heart** (Dicentra spectabilis)
- **Hosta** (Hosta hybrids)
- **Impatiens** (Impatiens walleriana)
- **Primrose** (Primula species)
- **Violet** (Viola species)
- **Virginia Bluebells** (Mertensia virginica)

color for late spring and summer. And when they're not in bloom, the juxtaposition of various colors and shapes of foliage will keep your displays interesting. Here are some ways to succeed with flowers in the shade:

■ HELP THE SOIL. If trees cause the shade, the roots may be sucking all the water and nutrients out of the general area. Even if the area is shady because of a looming fence or building, it may have poor soil. In any case, dig in some good organic matter to improve the area, being careful not to damage tree roots, especially of shallow-rooted species such as maples and river birch.

■ CONCENTRATE ON SPRINGTIME. There are many spring bulbs, groundcovers, and other flowering plants (such as woodland wildflowers) that are at their best early in the gardening year. Resolve to make a great show! Start the previous fall by putting in a variety of colorful bulbs.

■ UNDER TREES, USE POTS. Hang colorful potted plants from tree limbs (such as impatiens or tuberous begonias). Or place shade-tolerant flowers in pots here and there among the trees—on the ground, nestled among prominent roots, or tucked into the ground where there is enough room to dig. Just remember to keep these watered, fed, and groomed so they have a chance to look their best.

■ REDUCE THE GLOOM. If trees cause the shade, let in more light by removing lower limbs or thinning the canopy. You might even consider removing entire plants if they are really oppressive or overgrown. If a fence or hedge is keeping out light, see if you can remove or reduce its bulk.

While most flower-garden plants are sun lovers, many also bloom in shade, such as primrose.

COTTAGE GARDEN FAVORITES

Cottage gardens usually overflow with flowering herbaceous perennials, shrubs, annuals, herbs, and small flowering trees. A cottage garden is also a good place to use heirloom varieties. Try these:

- **Baby's Breath** (*Gypsophila paniculata*)
- **Bellflower** (*Campanula* species)
- **Clematis** (*Clematis* hybrids)
- **Columbine** (*Aquilegia* species)
- **Delphinium** (*Delphinium elatum*)
- **Foxglove** (*Digitalis* species)
- **Hollyhock** (*Alcea rosea*)
- **Hydrangea** (*Hydrangea macrophylla*)
- **Japanese Anemone** (*Anemone × hybrida*)
- **Lavender** (*Lavandula angustifolia*)
- **Lupine** (*Lupinus perennis*)
- **Mock Orange** (*Philadelphus coronarius*)
- **Pansy** (*Viola × wittrockiana*)
- **Peony** (*Paeonia* hybrids)
- **Phlox** (*Phlox* species)
- **Poppy** (*Papaver orientale*)
- **Pinks** (*Dianthus* species)
- **Roses** (*Rosa* hybrids)
- **Sweet Pea** (*Lathyrus* species)
- **Valerian** (*Centranthus ruber*)

Cottage Gardens

This classic English garden style has been in vogue for a long time throughout Europe, but has also captured the imaginations of American gardeners. It is such an appealing, romantic approach to gardening—a lush, somewhat disordered yard overflowing with colorful flowers.

Generally speaking, a cottage garden is a smallish space that does not appear "designed," though it does take planning. It should be informal but not messy. Plants are well tended, but they are allowed to express their natural exuberance. If sweet peas smother the fence, so be it; if the rose bush drapes over a garden ornament, no matter; if foxgloves seed about, they are allowed to flourish wherever they have found a footing. A cottage garden lacks some of the restrictions of other garden styles, and is allowed to evolve. It combines whatever you like and whatever works in your climate or garden situation—perennials, annuals, vines, flowering shrubs, herbs, and roses are all welcome in a cottage plot. The result is a delightful, colorful garden that looks informal yet welcoming.

Include a variety of plants. A typical cottage garden has a lush array of plants, of all flower and plant forms and textures. The trick is to use this variety without making it look too busy. Use the same design principles discussed earlier in the chapter to make your cottage garden look "at home." Roses and fragrant plants are also typical additions to this type of garden.

CAN'T MISS TIP:

FORMAL HELP

Certain non-plant elements can help your displays look more formal. Use elegant pots and urns, and place these prominently. As with plant placement in a formal garden, strive for symmetry and balance. Classic statuary, a fountain, or a reflecting pool can add style, class, and a sense of serenity. An enclosing wrought-iron fence or gate will also add formal charm.

Formal Gardens

Particularly if you have a formal-looking house—but even if you garden around a neat little bungalow—a formal garden can be appropriate, and your taste might naturally lean that way. Formal-looking gardens confer elegance and calm. So it stands to reason that they are not "busy" or heavily planted with a wide variety of flowers. A collection of less formal plants, however, can be made to seem more formal by planting them within a strict boundary, such as a low boxwood hedge.

Formal flower gardens are bounded by the strong lines of pathways, fences, and neatly clipped hedges of boxwood, laurel, yew, or some other evergreen that lends itself well to shearing. Within these, flower plantings are generally simple; typically there are blocks of one type of plant, often in a single color. Sometimes they are chosen to match or complement the house color. And white never goes out of style, always looking splendid against the green shrubbery that is the foundation of so many formal gardens. No matter how many flowers you plant or where, strive for symmetry and balance.

A formal garden typically has a limited plant palette, symmetry, and defined borders, such as walkways and clipped hedges.

Cut-Flower Gardens

Growing your own bouquets can add a satisfying element to flower gardening. So that you are not always depleting your flower borders, it can make

FORMAL FAVORITES

These are some flowers often seen in formal garden settings.

- **Astilbe** (*Astilbe* hybrids and cultivars)
- **Camellia** (*Camellia japonica*)
- **Daffodil** (*Narcissus* species and hybrids)
- **Foxglove** (*Digitalis purpurea*)
- **Hosta** (*Hosta* cultivars)
- **Impatiens** (*Impatiens walleriana*)
- **Iris** (*Iris* species)
- **Lavender** (*Lavandula angustifolia* and others)
- **Lily** (*Lilium* species)
- **Lupine** (*Lupinus* hybrids)
- **Monkshood** (*Aconitum napellus*)
- **Mountain Laurel** (*Kalmia latifolia*)
- **Mum** (*Dendranthema* hybrids)
- **Primrose** (*Primula* species)
- **Rose** (*Rosa* hybrids)
- **Sedum** (*Sedum* species, taller types)
- **Summer Phlox** (*Phlox paniculata*)
- **Tulip** (*Tulipa* hybrids)

Gladiolus has been a popular cut-flower plant for generations. Stagger the plantings of corms so that you have blooms over a longer period.

sense to set up an area devoted solely to flower production. This need not be a large area and it can still be colorful and pretty. However, because you are raising the plants to harvest the blooms, a cut-flower garden looks more like a vegetable garden, with plants grouped or in rows. To keep it looking tidy, make the edges clean and defined or install a low, decorative fence. Cut flowers, like any crop, thrive in good, fertile soil with no obstructions or weeds to inhibit their growth. For more information on cut flowers and bouquets, see Chapter 4.

For the best results, try some or all of these techniques:

■ SET ASIDE AN AREA IN FULL SUN. Most bouquet-type flowers are sun-lovers.

■ START SMALL. A few square feet will get you started; you can expand later after you find out how much effort this project takes and how many cut flowers you need.

■ GROW PLANTS WITH LONG CUTTING STEMS (not dwarf or compact varieties). Stake or otherwise support them while they are growing, so flower stalks grow straight and flowers don't wind up face down in the dirt after a hard rain.

■ SPACE THE PLANTS AT INTERVALS so that they are not crowded, and so they will grow well and straight. If you are not sure how much space a certain flower needs, err on the side of caution and give it plenty of room.

■ MULCH to keep invading weeds at bay, cool the soil, and keep moisture in the soil.

■ WATER DILIGENTLY. Flower buds and flowers on the verge of opening need regular, consistent water so they don't become distorted and so they have their best color. Water at the root zone as much as possible, rather than watering from overhead and getting the tops of the plants wet.

■ PICK EARLY AND OFTEN. Don't wait till the flowers are fully open; the best bouquets have flowers that are just about to open, so the show can be savored indoors. In addition, frequent picking inspires the plants to generate more buds.

- REPLENISH YOUR PLANTINGS. If an individual plant peters out or goes to seed, replace it with fresh reinforcements. You can plan ahead by starting seeds in staggered batches, or planting plants (or corms, as with gladiolus) at regular intervals, throughout the growing season.

Butterfly Gardens

It's so enchanting, the first time you see a butterfly flitting its merry way through your yard and coming to rest on one of your flowers. To make sure this is not just a happy accident, you can deliberately plant flowers that butterflies prefer (in both their caterpillar stage and their showy adult state) to assure their company throughout the summer. They're not just decorative, of course: Butterflies help pollinate your flowers as they feed.

A garden alive with insects such as butterflies is also a healthy place. Planting "monocultures" of lawn grass and foundation shrubs, as well as overusing garden chemicals, diminishes animal populations and limits their habitats. A garden full of flowers is not just a pretty sight, but is a sanctuary for wildlife. Plants that draw adult butterflies in scores include the following:

- BLAZING STAR (*Liatris spicata*)
- BUTTERFLY BUSH (*Buddleia davidii*)
- BUTTERFLY WEED (*Asclepias tuberosa*)
- CONEFLOWER (*Echinacea purpurea*)
- LANTANA (*Lantana camara*)
- MARIGOLD (*Tagetes* species)
- NEW ENGLAND ASTER (*Aster novae-angliae*)
- PENTAS (*Pentas lanceolata*)
- PINCUSHION FLOWER (*Scabiosa columbaria*)
- SUMMER PHLOX (*Phlox paniculata*)
- VERBENA (*Verbena canadensis*)
- ZINNIA (*Zinnia elegans*)

Tropical Scenes

This adventurous garden style has left the torrid tropics and made its way into the fancies of North American gardeners (as it once swept Victorian England). We can use tropical or exotic plants to get this effect, but may have to pamper them

CATERPILLARS, TOO!

If you really want to keep beautiful butterflies around, plan to accommodate them at their caterpillar stage as well. Caterpillar plants include milkweed, butterfly weed, fennel, parsley, Dutchman's pipe, passionflower, spicebush, pawpaw, and rue.

Butterflies are especially attracted to plants with numerous blooms clustered together, such as summer phlox. Daisy, zinnia, star-cluster, and lantana are also popular butterfly flowers.

Some plants lend a tropical feel to a garden, with large, brightly colored blooms or bold foliage.

indoors in the cold months, or consider them annuals. It often makes sense to grow some of them in pots, which has the advantages of letting you move them around to fine-tune your garden composition, and enjoy them indoors as cold-season houseplants. The basic idea is to use hot colors and bold textures—liberally, extravagantly!

Here are some popular plants for this use. Note that some of them have attractive, colorful foliage as well.

■ ANGEL'S TRUMPET (*Brugmansia arborea*)
■ BEGONIA (*Begonia* species and hybrids)
■ CANNA (*Canna* × *generalis*)
■ CROCOSMIA (*Crocosmia* species and hybrids)
■ DAHLIA (*Dahlia* hybrids)
■ HIBISCUS (*Hibiscus* species)
■ LANTANA (*Lantana* species and hybrids)
■ NASTURTIUM (*Tropaeolum majus*)
■ NEW GUINEA IMPATIENS (*Impatiens hawkeri*)
■ OLEANDER (*Nerium oleander*)
■ PASSIONFLOWER (*Passiflora caerulea*)
■ PRINCESS FLOWER (*Tibouchina urvilleana*)
■ SALVIA (*Salvia splendens*)

That Extra Touch

A garden is more than an artful gathering of plants; it is also a place to stroll, relax, and socialize. It can benefit from the inclusion of objects, both practical and decorative. These items make a garden more beautiful and more enjoyable. You don't want clutter, but a few carefully considered extras will make a world of difference, adding focal points, a sense of order, and personality. They'll also give your garden your own personal stamp.

Containers

Aside from what you might choose to grow in a container, the pot itself can become a significant garden element. Buy a pretty container, or paint or otherwise decorate one. It's wise to keep a collection of decorative pots around, and move them in and out of the garden or your patio displays as needed. This includes urns, pots, baskets, troughs, planter boxes, window boxes, and hanging baskets.

One brightly colored container can make a big difference! It can make the plants within it look even better. It can complete a garden picture by repeating and emphasizing flower colors from within it or nearby. Or it can tie a display to other colorful objects, from garden furniture to a decorative birdhouse to a fence or the house. And several brightly colored pots, clustered together, can set a color theme. So be bold, be daring, and above all have fun with container colors!

Ornaments

Careful placement of even the most ordinary objects can make a garden scene look artful and exciting, and add a finishing touch. Here are a few ideas.

- **SUNDIALS**: metal or bentwood, small or large, ornate or simple, practical or mostly decorative
- **STATUARY**: human figures, animals, abstract sculptures
- **FOUNTAINS**: ones that trickle, ones that spray into the air
- **TILES**: embedded in walls, in a terrace surface, on shelves, under or around potted plants
- **GAZING GLOBES**: now available in every color of the rainbow; nestled among flowers or raised on a pedestal
- **BIRDHOUSES**: small or large, purely decorative or actually practical; attached to walls, fences, trees, hanging in trees or from a porch
- **BIRD BATHS**: simple or ornate, colorful or plain; visiting birds will add life and movement to the garden

Garden Furnishings

A place to sit, or better still, dine outdoors, is always welcome. It allows you to enjoy the fruits of your labors, to savor your flowers at different times of the day, in almost every season. Style and color in garden furniture can set a tone or further a theme.

- **BENCHES**: from pine to teak to wrought iron; plain, weathered, or painted; with or without colorful cushions
- **CHAIRS**: wooden or wrought iron, new or salvaged, plain or painted, with or without colorful cushions
- **TABLE AND CHAIR SETS**: in many materials and styles; try to pick something compatible with the style of your garden and home, and in scale with your yard or the corner you are tucking it into
- **UMBRELLAS, HAMMOCKS, HANGING CHAIRS**: on temporary summer display, plain or colorful

A garden is more than an artful gathering of plants; it is also a place to stroll, relax, and socialize.

Bringing Flowers
Indoors

One of the greatest pleasures of growing your own flowers is harvesting them for bouquets. Even the process is deeply enjoyable, as you putter around the yard with your clippers, admiring what's in bloom and making choices about what to cut today. This is your reward for nurturing the flowers in your yard.

Ideally, you would wish any blossom you grow to be appropriate for a bouquet. But some flowers are better than others, either because they hold their blooms well (without wilting or shattering right away) or because they have good strong stems to support the flowers. To make the process even more fulfilling, you should grow a great variety of flowers. If you'd like to raise flowers specifically for flower arranging, you can devote a portion of your yard, preferably in full sun and good, fertile soil, to a cutting garden.

A big benefit to cutting bouquets is that you are, in effect, deadheading, or taking off blossoms before they have a chance to mature past their prime. Left on the plant, of course, they eventually fade and either hang there limply or fall off, while the parts remaining on the stem get busy developing seeds or forming fruit (a process sometimes called "going to seed"). Seed development takes a lot of energy, and if your plants reach this point, they'll start diverting all their energy into this process and flower production will slow and eventually stop. So, cut away!

A bouquet of flowers, whether large or small, brings your enjoyment of the garden indoors.

FORCING BRANCHES

Impatient for spring? Good news! Those bare-limbed woody plants in your yard can give you an early show. You can start cutting branches on certain flowering trees and shrubs after the first of the year in most climates, although the closer it is to actual blooming time, the faster the branches will come into full flower.

1. Using sharp clippers, make a neat cut on the base of the branch. Then use a sharp knife to split the stem about an inch to increase water uptake.
2. Completely immerse the branch in lukewarm to warm water overnight to soften the bud scales. Depending on the branch's length, a pail, the kitchen sink, or even a tub will do.
3. In the morning, stand the stems in a bucket or vase. Store in a room with relatively cool temperatures (60 degrees Fahrenheit—still much warmer than outside!) and out of direct sunlight.
4. Change the water once a week.
5. When the buds begin to show color, you can bring the branches into the house and make an arrangement, alone or with florist flowers.

The best pruners for cutting stems for arrangements are bypass types (left), rather than anvil pruners (right), which can damage stems.

Getting Started: Making the Cut

Begin by taking a bucket of water out into the garden with you. (Forget those romantic images of carrying them in a basket or the crook of your arm!) Most flowers can't be deprived of moisture for long before they begin to show signs of distress, including wilting and dropping petals. The bucket needs only a few inches of tepid water in the bottom, so it's not heavy and doesn't slosh. You just want to give each cut stem a temporary drink until you can get it indoors.

Although you may be in the habit of snapping or tearing off flower stems, it's not a good practice because you're damaging both the bouquet stem and the plant that remains behind as well. Nor are household scissors or blade-and-anvil clippers the way to go, because they mash stems. Instead, use a good, sharp tool intended for gardening. (See box, "The Best Cutting Tools," page 67, for your options.) Cut stems as long as possible (you can always shorten them later), promptly drop each one into the bucket, and keep moving.

As for the sort of cut you should make, there are two kinds:

- **SLANTED CUTS:** These are appropriate for annuals and perennials, which have flexible herbaceous stems. A slanted cut exposes more stem area, maximizing water uptake.
- **SQUARE CUTS:** Use these for woody stems, such as stems from flowering shrubs, woody vines, or trees. Later, indoors, you're going to split their pith to increase water uptake, so the initial flat cut is fine.
- **MORE CUTTING ADVICE:** Don't make a point of getting foliage with your cut stems; you'll only be stripping them off indoors and discarding them. It's much better to leave them on the plant, where they can keep growing and helping to nourish the plant, so it will keep producing flowers for you.

Once your bucket is full, it's time to come inside and re-cut the stems. Work in the kitchen by the sink. Strip off and discard leaves, especially those that would end up underwater in a vase (they'll only decay and cloud the water,

CAN'T MISS TIP:

FLOWERS TO FORCE

Flowering shrubs and trees that respond well to forcing include:

- **Cornelian Cherry** (*Cornus mas*)
- **Daphne** (*Daphne odorata*)
- **Forsythia** (*Forsythia × intermedia*)
- **Rhododendron** (*Rhododendron* species)
- **Spicebush** (*Lindera benzoin*)
- **Willow** (*Salix* species)
- **Flowering Quince** (*Chaenomeles* species)
- **Witch Hazel** (*Hamamelis* species)

Top: Strip off lower leaves that will be under water in the vase.
Center: Recut stems of herbaceous plants under water.
Bottom: Split or mash the ends of woody stems.

shortening the life of the entire arrangement). Remove any thorns as well (there is a special tool made for removing thorns from stems, available from garden and florist supply companies).

Fill the sink with a few inches of tepid water, or use an "underwater stem cutter," a nifty gadget available from florist supply houses. Hold the stems in the water while re-cutting (on a slant, again, for most). A sharp knife is fine. The object is to remove stem calluses and air bubbles that might have developed while the stems were in the bucket outside and to encourage the stem's water-conducting cells to fill up. In the case of woody stems, split the stem/pith upward about an inch; this exposes even more plant cells that will take up water.

When to Cut?

To a certain extent, it's a matter of taste regarding when in a flower's development you should harvest it for use in an arrangement. But if you pick while it's still in bud, it may never open. On the other hand, if you wait too long and pick when a flower is fully open, its life in a vase may be short. Your best bet is to cut when buds are swelling and you can see the petal color. If a blossom is clasped by a calyx (the green protective wrapping around some buds), it should be showing signs of peeling away or loosening its grip.

THE BEST CUTTING TOOLS

No matter what tool you choose, the cutting surfaces should be clean (no dirt, no gummed up sap) so your cuts are neat and don't spread disease. And, of course, the blades should be sharp. The most fastidious bouquet-pickers wear gloves.

- **Sharp Knife:** A Swiss army knife, steak knife, or anything similar, will do, so long as the cutting edge is not roughly serrated.

- **Garden Pruners:** Ordinary lightweight pruners generally do a good job. Use the scissors/bypass type rather than anvil pruners.

- **Butterfly-Handled Japanese Shears:** The ones with soft vinyl handles are wonderful. Plus, left-handed people can use these, too.

- **Cut-and-Hold Clippers:** Upon cutting, these clever clippers hold the stem for you until you take it out. Very convenient when you're reaching far into a bush or flower border and don't want to drop any cut stems.

- **Pruning Snips:** Stainless-steel cutting blades and ambidextrous cushion grips make for comfortable cutting.

SPECIAL CASES

Not every flower can be treated in the standard manner. A few have special requirements to become long-lasting bouquet flowers.

- **Daffodils and other spring bulbs:** Often there is a pale green or white section at the very bottom of the stem; this should be cut off, as it won't take up water.

- **Delphiniums, dahlias, other hollow-stemmed flowers:** Turn the stem upside down and gingerly drip water into it as though you were filling a straw, then plug the end with a tiny bit of cotton ball before putting it back in the water upright.

- **Poppies, heliotrope, other sap-producing flowers:** Stop sap from dripping by sealing the re-cut stem end, either by holding it for a few seconds to a lit match or candle, or dipping it into boiling water for thirty seconds.

Some stems need support, such as a wrapping of wax paper, while the plants are being readied for use in arrangements.

For flowers that bloom in spikes, generally speaking, the older blossoms are toward the base and open first. In those cases, you must strike a compromise, cutting when some of these are already open but the smaller ones near the top are not yet unfurled. Blazing-star is one exception, opening its flowers from the top down; cut these stalks when they are showing color about halfway down.

While you can cut bouquet flowers any time of the day that is convenient for you, certain times are preferable. Early morning after the dew has dried is perfect. Midday is stressful because at that hour the plants are losing more moisture than they are taking up and therefore are much more prone to wilting upon picking. Evening is also fine, though the plant's moisture is not at its peak. Alternatively, any cool, cloudy day is good.

Conditioning

Immediately after you've re-cut the stems, put the flowers in a clean container of water. The water temperature should be cool—not cold, not too warm. Fill it up only about halfway; more is unnecessary. Next, mist the entire bouquet with a gentle spray.

The actual conditioning process is meant to let each flower stem absorb water. In the process, the stomata (pores in the stems and leaves, invisible to the eye) will close up, which reduces water loss later. This process is most successful in darkness, so now is the time to move the entire bouquet into a cool, dark place. Professional florists, of course, use a refrigerator or walk-in cooler, but if that's not possible for you, a cool basement or other dim room is fine.

Some flowers need support while being conditioned or their stems will arch or twist and turn. Tulips and gerberas are particularly prone to this problem. Luckily, it's easily solved. Just roll individual stems, or several together, in several sheets of newspaper or wax paper, fastened with rubber bands, then set them in water and condition as described earlier.

Certain other flowers absorb water through their blossoms as well as their stems, and should be immersed completely for an hour or so after harvesting. Hydrangeas, violets, and lilies are examples. Afterwards, set their stems in water and continue the conditioning process.

Aftercare

Once your flowers are conditioned, you're ready to arrange them. Most do best in fresh, cool water; you can stir in a preservative at the outset if you wish (see "Bouquet Preservatives" below). Here are some final tips for prolonging the vase life of your homegrown bouquets:

■ CHANGE THE WATER DAILY. Dump it all out and rinse the vase, then refill. Cool or lukewarm water is easier for the stems to absorb. Re-cut the stems before returning them to the vase if you wish or if they are beginning to look bad.

■ MIST THE BOUQUET lightly once a day or more often. This makes a remarkable difference!

■ DISPLAY THE BOUQUET in a location out of direct, hot sunlight.

■ STORE THE BOUQUET at night (or when nobody is around to see it) in a cool, dark room or the refrigerator.

■ REMOVE FLOWERS PROMPTLY as they fade or wilt (foliage, too, if any).

Bouquet Preservatives

It's optional, but many flower arrangers like to add some sort of preservative to the vase water. There are plenty of "homemade" options, but their effectiveness is questionable (among these are a penny, an aspirin tablet, a splash of vodka, a drop of bleach). Florists use commercial preparations, which come in small packets in the form of a white powder. These prevent bacterial infections and provide a few nutrients. Once stirred in (*before* the flowers are put in!), they seem to keep the water clearer and help the flowers look good longer. You can buy these packets at greenhouse-supply shops or obtain a few from your local florist for free or a small fee.

There is no need to keep adding more to the vase each day. Use the preservative on the first day only, and thereafter, just change the water daily.

Immediately after you've re-cut the stems, put the flowers in a clean container of water.

BOUQUET FAVORITES

Seed and nursery catalogs often devote entire sections to plants that they suggest for cutting. Here you can find all sorts of wonderful new colors or color combinations you may never see at a local garden center, which will give you fresh, exciting ideas and result in some bragging-rights bouquets! The following are some of the best (and easiest to grow) cut flowers.

Annuals:
Bachelor's Button (*Centaurea cyanus*)
Calendula (*Calendula officinalis*)
Cleome (*Cleome hassleriana*)
Cosmos (*Cosmos bipinnatus*)
Gloriosa Daisy (*Rudbeckia hirta*)
Larkspur (*Consolida ambigua*)
Snapdragon (*Antirrhinum majus*)
Stock (*Matthiola* species)
Sunflower (*Helianthus annuus*)
Sweet Pea (*Lathyrus odoratus*)
Zinnia (*Zinnia elegans*)

Perennials:
Baby's Breath (*Gypsophila paniculata*)
Black-Eyed Susan (*Rudbeckia fulgida*)
Blanket Flower (*Gaillardia × grandiflora*)
Columbine (*Aquilegia* species)
Coneflower (*Echinacea purpurea*)
Coreopsis (*Coreopsis* species)
Daisy (*Leucanthemum* species)

Delphinium (*Delphinium elatum*)
Lupine (*Lupinus perennis*)
Mum (*Dendranthema* hybrids)
Peony (*Paeonia* hybrids)
Perennial Sunflower (*Helianthus* species)
Pincushion Flower (*Scabiosa columbaria*)

Bulbs, Corms, and Tubers:
Daffodil (*Narcissus* hybrids)
Gladiolus (*Gladiolus* hybrids)
Lily (*Lilium* species)
Ornamental Onion (*Allium* species)
Tulip (*Tulipa* hybrids)

Flowering Shrubs:
Daphne (*Daphne × burkwoodii*)
Forsythia (*Forsythia × intermedia*)
Hydrangea (*Hydrangea* species)
Lilac (*Syringa vulgaris*)
Rose (*Rosa* hybrids)
Viburnum (*Viburnum* species)

Flower Arranging Simplified

After all this preparation, the great moment finally arrives: the arranging of a bouquet. Here are some general principles to get you started. As your confidence grows and your flower palette expands, you'll be making bigger and better arrangements. But it helps at the outset to understand and master the basics.

How to Choose a Vase

First of all, choose something that is practical. It should be able to hold water without leaking, obviously, but it should also be sturdy or balanced enough so that it won't topple once the bouquet is placed inside. Ideally, your bouquet will be in proportion to the height and heft of the container (in other words, don't insert a top-heavy arrangement). Vase color, or the lack of it (clear glass) is a matter of personal taste. However, the more varied the colors and types of flowers, the more important it is to keep the vessel simple, so it doesn't distract or detract. Plain glass vases or subtly tinted ones return the focus to the flowers, as do neutral-hued and white ceramic containers. On the other hand, a single-color bouquet can look splendid in a decorative, multi-colored vase, if one of the colors matches the flowers.

Pastel blues, pinks, and lavenders create a harmonious bouquet. A combination of bright oranges, reds, and yellows also works well.

Six Silhouettes

Professional florists use six basic arrangement shapes all the time, and you can easily adapt any of these to home use. The names sound technical, but the idea is really very simple—you are establishing the outline of your flower arrangement, the shape it appears to have when you step back and look at it.

- LINE: The first stem establishes a central axis, and all other stems are placed in and around it in symmetrical fashion. The resulting arrangement looks a bit sparse, but also attractively architectural.
- LINE-MASS: Same as line, except that the bulkier, larger flowers are kept close to the bottom of the bouquet (so the arrangement doesn't topple over).
- CIRCULAR AND TRIANGULAR: These start the same way as the two simpler styles above, but lighter flowers are filled in around the main axis, giving the overall shape or impression of the arrangement as either rounded or like a pointed-up triangle. Many homegrown bouquets are naturally circular, and look balanced this way.
- SQUARE AND FAN: Begin by cutting all flower stems the same length. For a square arrangement, array them vertically; for a fan, angle them outward. Either of these may require a base of floral foam ("Oasis™") material or marbles to sustain the shape.

Color Arranging

There are endless ways to combine flowers in arrangements. And there is certainly nothing wrong with simply collecting favorite flowers from the garden and putting them together in a vase. But to achieve a truly pleasing combination, you should pay some attention to certain design principles.

- HARMONY: Just as in your flowerbeds, color harmony is achieved by combining bold or primary colors with one another, or pastels or soft colors with one another.
- CONTRAST: Try making a simple one- or two-color bouquet and then injecting just one or two surprising colors. For instance, an arrange-

Flower arrangements can be complex, including a variety of textures, colors, and forms, or simple, such as this clutch of white peonies in an elegant vase.

ment of white and yellow flowers gains a jolt of excitement if you tuck in a stem or two of red flowers. Or a blue- and purple-themed bouquet gains dimension if you include a bit of bright yellow or hot pink as an accent.

■ SINGLE-COLOR BOUQUETS: These can be quite striking, but it's important not to overdo or the result, at least from across the room, will be a blob of sameness. Use fewer flowers and allow them a little "air" so they can be appreciated individually as well as collectively.

Design Tricks for Mixed Bouquets

As in the garden, variety is often best. But if you want more than a loose, informal bouquet, here are some techniques the professionals use to make their arrangements more appealing.

■ BIG FIRST: Place the largest, heaviest flowers in the vase first, and work around them, adding lighter ones or even greenery as filler.

■ REPETITION: To keep the bouquet from looking too busy, or haphazard, use the same color repeatedly, even if different types of flowers supply it.

■ OUT OF MANY, ONE: Use a clump of smaller flowers to create the same impression as one larger one.

■ BALANCE: It's not necessary to have a perfectly symmetrical bouquet; asymmetry can, in fact, be more pleasing, as long as there is balance.

Success with Drying Flowers

Another way to enjoy flowers from your garden is to preserve or dry them. You can then either make long-lasting arrangements, or use them for craft projects like wreaths or potpourri. A single dried flower stem tucked under a ribbon atop a wrapped gift is very nice, too!

Not all flowers lend themselves to this process, however. Their petals may be too frail and shatter, they may shrivel beyond recognition, or they may brown or spoil. The best candidates are ones with smaller or thinner durable petals, or blooms that are actually clusters of smaller flowers. These sorts are better able to hold their color and form well even when dried.

There are two ways to effectively dry flowers, one simple and low-tech, the other involving special supplies and more time. Either method may result in slightly faded flowers or a slight change in flower color, but the appearance can still be satisfying.

BEST FLOWERS FOR DRYING

- **Baby's Breath** (*Gypsophila paniculata*)
- **Bachelor's Button** (*Centaurea cyanus*)
- **Black-Eyed Susan** (*Rudbeckia* species)
- **Delphinium** (*Delphinium ajacis*)
- **Globe Thistle** (*Echinops ritro*)
- **Goldenrod** (*Solidago* species)
- **Gomphrena** (*Gomphrena globosa*)
- **Lavender** (*Lavandula* species)

- **Marigold** (*Tagetes* species)
- **Ornamental Onion** (*Allium* species)
- **Rose** (in bud, especially miniatures) (*Rosa* hybrids)
- **Salvia** (*Salvia* species)
- **Sedum** (especially 'Autumn Joy') (*Sedum* species)
- **Strawflower** (*Helichrysum bracteatum*)
- **Yarrow** (*Achillea* species)

Before you begin, pick the longest stems you can (because you may shorten them later). Collect them when the flowers are plump with moisture but not damp from dew or rain, ideally mid-morning or early evening. Whatever stage they are in—opening bud, semi-open blossom, fully open blossom—is how most will dry, with no change. Some flowers, like strawflower, do continue to open as they dry, so pick these just as the buds are opening; picking a fully open flower will result in a splayed-out bloom when it is finished drying.

Air Drying

Prepare space in a warm, dry room that has decent air circulation, such as a shed with a window, a screened-in porch, a dry basement, or an attic with

Many common garden flowers can be dried and used to make everlasting arrangements or wreaths.

an overhead fan. Any dampness or humidity will slow down or spoil the process, so make sure the room you choose is really dry and well ventilated. Bundle several stems together (five is a good number), tie with string or a rubber band, and hang upside down. Hang from a hook, nail, or peg, or along a coat hanger. Take care that the flowers are not crammed together; you can stagger them within the bundle or vary the stem lengths.

Check periodically to be sure the stems have not dried away from the string or rubber bands, slipped through, and fallen to the ground.

Alternatively, lay the flowers flat on a screen or sheet of newspaper, and gently turn them every few days. Make sure they don't touch or overlap. Air drying is complete in as little as a week or two, depending on the flower and the dryness of the room.

Using a Desiccant

First, buy the following supplies at a hobby store: a bag of silica gel (a white powder drying agent that absorbs moisture) and an airtight container such as a tin (Tupperware and the like let in light and are less desirable). Deeper containers, of course, will hold more flowers.

Sprinkle a thin layer of the silica gel in the bottom of the tin (half an inch is fine). Lay the blossoms neatly on top, taking care that they are not touching each other. Daisy-like flowers can be put in face down if you wish, many-petaled flowers can be face up, and all others can be laid flat. Using a spoon or cup, gently sprinkle additional silica gel over and around the flowers. Cover them completely, then add another half-inch for good measure. If the container is deep, you can then add another layer or two of flowers.

Tightly seal the container, label it with the contents and the date, and put in a cool, dark place where it will not be disturbed. Check every few days until you are satisfied that your flowers are fully dry. When you finally remove the flowers, sift off the remaining silica gel. If bits remain, blow them off or gently dust them off with a paintbrush. (You can reuse the silica gel again and again.)

Edible Flowers

When using whole flowers or individual petals, edible flowers add color and whimsy to food. They can be added to salads, cheese spreads, and herb butters; used to decorate summery drinks or punch; or sprinkled on ice cream, sorbet, cake frosting, and other sweet treats. At a brunch you may add them to the batter or use them as garnish for crepes or waffles. More ideas and good recipes can be found in many cookbooks, especially those that emphasize summer entertaining (when your garden flowers are in their prime!).

Always wash off the flowers when you bring them inside. Never serve flowers or flower parts that may have been exposed to garden chemicals. If you won't be using them immediately, keep the flowers in jars or bowls of water, or rolled in a damp paper towel and stashed in a sealed plastic bag. In either case, they'll stay fresher longer in the refrigerator.

Rose hips and petals can be used to make an herbal tea.

CAN'T MISS TIP:

THE TASTIEST FLOWERS

It is very important that you be completely certain of an edible flower's identity before you serve it. Some of the best flowers for eating are:

- **Bee Balm** (*Monarda didyma*)
- **Calendula** (*Calendula officinalis*)
- **Chives** (*Allium schoenoprasum*)
- **Daylily** (especially the buds) (*Hemerocallis* hybrids)
- **Lavender** (*Lavandula* species)
- **Nasturtium** (*Tropaeolum majus*)
- **Pansy** (*Viola × wittrockiana*)
- **Rose** (*Rosa* hybrids)

Edible flowers, such as calendula, make beautiful additions to salads, desserts, and other foods.

Can't Miss Flower Favorites

beautiful flowers spring from many types of plants, from annuals to bulbs to perennials. And let's not forget the blooms that adorn flowering shrubs, smaller ornamental trees, and vines and climbers. Low, high, and in between, it is possible to decorate every corner of your yard. But where to begin, how to choose?

In this chapter, you will find helpful profiles of many choices, spanning the categories mentioned. Obviously, this is but a sampling of all that the plant world has to offer. But the ones on this list are special. To assure gardening success, they have been tried and tested, passing muster on the following key criteria:

- Attractive flowers
- Dependable performance
- Easy care
- Wide availability

Viola
(*Viola cornuta*)

The following entries are intended to get you started, to guide you in your choices—and to inspire you. Have fun choosing and shopping for the ones that appeal to you, and be open to making changes or exploring further options in the future. This directory is simply meant to open the garden gate and welcome you into the delightful world of flower gardening.

KEY TO ICONS

Along with each plant entry, you will notice small graphic icons. They convey additional useful information about the plant's characteristics or benefits. There are also icons indicating light requirements.

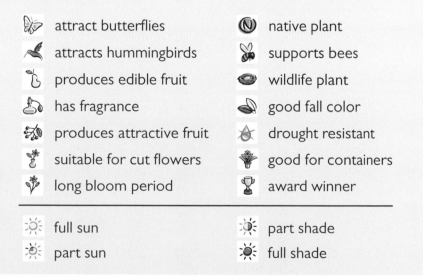

attract butterflies   native plant

attracts hummingbirds   supports bees

produces edible fruit   wildlife plant

has fragrance   good fall color

produces attractive fruit   drought resistant

suitable for cut flowers   good for containers

long bloom period   award winner

full sun   part shade

part sun   full shade

Winning Plants

In some of the entries to follow, you will find that a certain plant, or a particular selection of it, has won an award. This is a great place to start your hunt for the best of the best.

AAS: All-America Selections

Commonly awarded to annuals (and vegetable varieties), this honor is bestowed on an elite group of plants each year. They were grown in trial gardens nationwide and evaluated by experts, usually beating out many competitors. The award signals that a plant has not only been judged excellent in the context of its peers, but is widely adaptable. To learn more, visit the website at **www.allamericaselections.org**.

PPA: Perennial Plant Association

Only one plant wins Perennial Plant of the Year each year, after being nominated and winning the most votes from a group of experts. Members of the association are nursery owners and staffers; growers and hybridizers; and other professionals who develop, raise, and market perennials to the American public. They know their plants! To learn more, visit the website at **www.perennialplant.org**.

Glossary of Flower Terms

Some of the following entries include terms that may be unfamiliar to you, but are in common use not only in gardening books, but on nursery tags and in plant-catalog descriptions as well.

Bract: a showy leaf at the base of a flower or group of flowers, not always green. On some plants the bracts are showier than the actual flowers (as with the flowering dogwood).

Bulb: a swollen structure consisting of leaves, a flower bud or buds for the next season's bloom, and a short basal plate of tissue that is the plant's stem.

Corm: not actually a bulb, though it resembles one. Modified stem tissue that remains underground, storing energy for the plant above.

Cultivar: short for "cultivated variety," it refers to a plant that was selected for desirable characteristics such as flower color, bloom size, or attractive, distinctive foliage. The plant has been given its own, often descriptive, name,

Ornamental Onion
(*Allium sphaerocephalum*)

and will maintain its uniqueness when propagated (typically by cuttings or division, since many do not "come true" from seed).

Deadhead: the practice of removing spent flowers. This subverts a plant's natural tendency to begin going to seed/forming fruit. Instead, a deadheaded plant tends to redirect that energy into producing still more flowers.

Disk Flowers: the center, or cone, of daisies and similar flowers. Disk flowers are actually a compact group of small, tube-shaped flowers.

Flower Head: a group of flowers that are arranged in various types of clusters; some look like one big flower at a glance or from a distance. A daisy is actually a cluster of small flowers, and so are lantana and sedum.

Hybrid: a cross between two related species, either in the same genus or the same plant family. Sometimes naturally occurring, but most often created by intentional transference of pollen from one plant to another to create seeds containing the genes from both parents.

Palmate: leaves with leaflets arranged like spokes on a wheel.

Panicle: a group of flowers arranged on a branched stem.

Pinnate: leaves with leaflets arranged on either side of a stalk, like a ladder (*pinna* is Latin for "feather").

Raceme: a group of flowers arranged on a central, or single, stalk with the youngest flowers at the tip. Each flower is connected to the stem by a pedicel.

Ray Flowers: on daisies and related plants, the showy outer ring of flowers, which are usually thought of as the petals, or outer petals.

Rhizome: a swollen stem structure, sometimes below ground (as with trillium and Solomon's seal) and sometimes at the surface (as with bearded iris).

Spike: an arrangement of flowers on a plant where the individual florets are attached directly to the main, central stem.

Sucker: a shoot growing from a plant's roots (or the underground part of the stem). These are a natural growth habit for plants that form a grove of stems (some shrubs are referred to as "suckering"). At the base of trees they should be clipped off, as they weaken a plant by sapping energy. Out-of-place, upright growing stems from the branches of trees are called "water sprouts."

Taproot: the central, primary root of a plant. Often thicker and longer than the others, it can hold reserve moisture to help the plant survive dry times. Most plants with large taproots do not like to be moved once established.

Tuber: a structure that looks like an odd-shaped (not round) bulb, but is a swollen, underground stem modified to store food energy for the plant.

Umbel: a flower cluster that is globe-shaped or flat-topped, and is composed of florets arranged on short stalks emanating from a single central point.

Red Buckeye
(*Aesculus* × *carnea*)

Annuals and Bedding Plants

For sheer flower power, annuals are hard to beat. Because their entire life cycle must be completed in one growing season—which is the technical definition of the word "annual"—these plants work fast. If you grow them from seed, you can start them indoors in late winter or early spring, get them outdoors after the last frost, and expect blooms shortly thereafter. If you buy plants, individually or in flats, at the local garden center the results are even quicker because the foliage and often the flowers are already up and running.

Modern-day annuals have been bred to produce copious quantities of flowers, or lush foliage, throughout the growing season. They rush to flowering because their means of reproducing themselves is by seed. And to get there, the flowers must come first. This great output guarantees bountiful garden color, and also makes most annuals great for bouquets. By the time fall comes and the seeds form (if they do, before frost), the plants are spent and die. But by then, you've certainly gotten your money's worth! Many annuals should be routinely deadheaded so they will not complete the cycle of forming seed before the season is over. Some plants are actually perennial in some regions, but are used as annuals in other areas because they are not hardy there. For instance, lantana can be a perennial in the southern parts of the country, but is used as an annual further north. Some tropical plants are also commonly used for temporary display.

African Daisy
Osteospermum species
MATURE HEIGHT × WIDTH: 1-2 feet × 2-4 feet
FLOWER COLORS: yellow, white, pink, lavender, purple
FLOWER SIZE: 2-3 inches
SOIL: average to dry, well drained

Quite possibly the easiest daisies you'll ever grow! Originally from South Africa, these perky favorites are at their best in long, hot, dry summers. The plants stretch and sprawl and are studded with purple-eyed flowers for months on end.

Because they flower so thickly, African daisies are often used in mass plantings. (In California, they are such a popular roadside plant that many people know them as "freeway daisies.") They're ideal for slopes, banks, curbside plantings, as an edging, or along paths. Get a tidier show in your garden simply by pinching back the tips to encourage more compact growth. You might also enjoy growing them in smaller doses, as in a hanging basket or as dependable color in a mixed bed. Plants labeled as *Dimorphotheca* are the same or similar species (some species once in the genus *Dimorphotheca* have been moved to *Osteospermum*).

GOOD CHOICES: Passion Mix (shades of pink and lavender) was a 1999 AAS winner; deep purple 'African Queen'; 'White Cloud'

Angelonia
Angelonia angustifolia
MATURE HEIGHT × WIDTH: 1-2 feet × 1 foot
FLOWER COLORS: purple, pink, white, and bicolors
FLOWER SIZE: 1 inch
SOIL: moist, well drained

Characterized by one horticulturist as "snapdragons on steroids," angelonia is a relatively new sight at garden centers and is certainly a step up from that old standby. Originally hailing from tropical and subtropical Central and South America, this handsome plant can be grown in a bed or container. Its habit is bushy and upright, with rich flower colors and excellent basal branching. Overall, they are tidy and formal in appearance, though some types are more prone than others to cascading over on their sides (which can be a benefit when grown in a pot). Angelonia thrives in warm, sunny conditions and well-drained, fertile soil. From late spring to fall its stems are adorned with racemes of flowers up to 8 inches long, and it does not require deadheading to continue blooming.

GOOD CHOICES: deep plum 'Carita', Angel Mist Series

ANNUALS AND BEDDING PLANTS

Bachelor's Button
Centaurea cyanus
MATURE HEIGHT × WIDTH: 1-3 feet × 4-8 inches
FLOWER COLORS: purple, blue, white, pink, maroon
FLOWER SIZE: 1 inch
SOIL: average to dry

Pretty, jaunty bachelor's button, also called cornflower, blooms well from spring until the high heat of summer sets in. The small but durable flowers are held aloft on wiry but flexible stems that toss in the breeze. Because the blossoms are slow to "shatter" (drop their petals), they last a long time, whether outdoors in your garden or indoors in a vase. This quality makes them a nice ingredient in casual homegrown bouquets, fresh or dried.

Bachelor's buttons are a popular ingredient in wildflower meadow mixes, but you can also tuck a few plants into an informal flower border. They prosper in full sun and need little care and always provide an enthusiastic and dependable show. The species is blue flowered, but there are a variety of other colors, usually found in mixes. They typically will reseed and seedlings will pop up the next spring, often in drier areas of the garden.

GOOD CHOICES: Florence Series has many hues; 'Blue Boy' is an especially vivid blue variety

California Poppy
Eschscholzia californica
MATURE HEIGHT × WIDTH: 8-12 inches × 12 inches
FLOWER COLORS: orange, red, pink, yellow, white
FLOWER SIZE: 3 inches
SOIL: average, well drained

The state flower of California, this splendid bloomer is readily available and easy to grow. The orange species is still one of the finest sources of luminous, pure garden orange—grow some plants in the company of any blue flower for a stunning picture. Or try the beautiful cultivars, in many other hues, which are easy from seed and are listed in many mail-order catalogs.

To succeed, California poppy needs only full sun and decent soil. If it likes your garden, it will self-sow in the coming years. The foliage is grayish-green, ferny, and rather succulent, which helps the plants endure dry spells. It can get a bit sprawling and raggedy late in the season, at which point you can pull out the plants and look forward to next year's show.

GOOD CHOICES: Thai Silk Series has ruffled petals in red, pink, yellow, and orange; 'Purple Gleam' is actually soft-colored, rose to lavender; 'White Linen' is the finest pure white

Cleome
Cleome hassleriana
MATURE HEIGHT × WIDTH: 3-5 feet × 1-2 feet
FLOWER COLORS: pink, lavender, rose, white
FLOWER SIZE: 1-2 inches
SOIL: light, fertile, well drained

Because the stems are tall and the flower clusters atop them are so spectacular (4 to 6 inches across), cleome plants are a dramatic, substantial addition to any flower display. They're a great source of dependable consistent color in a border where other plants are coming in and out of bloom over the course of the summer. The airy flowers have a "spidery" look, hence the other common name of spider flower. As the flowers wave in the summer breeze, they draw butterflies and hummingbirds to your garden.

Cleome is very easy to grow. Just plant the seeds or seedlings in warm soil in early summer, water regularly, and they will take off. Once established, they require little care. At the end of the season, they will drop plenty of seeds, so if you don't want lots of the plants in your garden next year, deadhead before they begin to fade—or better yet, cut some stems for lively bouquets.

GOOD CHOICES: soft pink 'Sparkler Blush' was a 2002 AAS winner; 'Lavender Sparkler' and 'White Sparkler' are also good choices

Cosmos
Cosmos bipinnatus
MATURE HEIGHT × WIDTH: 2-5 feet × 1-2 feet
FLOWER COLORS: pink, red, white, lavender
FLOWER SIZE: 3 inches
SOIL: average, well drained

With their delicate, divided, feathery green foliage and profusion of daisy-like blossoms, cosmos are guaranteed to bring lots of easy-going cheer to your summer garden. You can grow tall ones toward the back of a bed (planted close together, they shouldn't need staking), or choose dwarf varieties (2 to 3 feet tall) to slip in anywhere or to pretty up container displays. They come in many hues in the white-pink-purple range and look wonderful mixed together. A related species, *Cosmos sulphureus*, has yellow to orange flowers; there are also hybrids of the two species.

Just make sure your cosmos plants get plenty of sun. Average, well-drained soil is best; rich, fertile soil seems to make them floppy and to inspire more foliage than flowers.

GOOD CHOICES: Sea Shells Mix has pastel hues and unusual fluted petals; the Sonata Series are excellent dwarf varieties; 'White Sonata' is an outstanding dwarf white

Fan Flower
Scaevola aemula
MATURE HEIGHT × WIDTH: 6 inches-2 feet × 4-5 feet
FLOWER COLORS: lilac, purple, white
FLOWER SIZE: ¹/₂-1 inch
SOIL: average to moist, well drained

Justly popular as a hanging-basket plant, fan flower is a full, lush grower that showers itself in dainty flowers for most of the summer. The botanical name comes from the Latin *scaeva*, which means "left-handed"—which refers to the unique hand- or fan-shaped form of the small flowers. The plant is at its best in average soil, with regular watering, and with a spot in full or dappled sunshine. If you don't want to grow it in a basket, try it in a window box, as part of a mixed display in a larger pot, or as a groundcover edging a border. Expect to get plenty of color for very little effort.

Traditionally found in blue, lilac-blue, and purple, fan flower is now also seen in pink and white. Mixing several hues together can make a fine display.

GOOD CHOICES: 'Blue Wonder' is the best, non-fading blue

Flowering Tobacco
Nicotiana alata
MATURE HEIGHT × WIDTH: 1-4 feet × 1-3 feet
FLOWER COLORS: white, greenish, pink, red, purple
FLOWER SIZE: 2 inches
SOIL: average to fertile, well drained

Yes, this plant really is related to tobacco, the crop. However, its attraction is its carefree beauty. Trumpet-shaped blossoms of many different, appealing colors adorn the tall, somewhat lanky plants. Often the flowers are sweetly scented, even more so in the evening hours when moths may come by. During the day, you may also spot visiting hummingbirds.

Flowering tobacco is a nice choice for mixing in with other flowers. The chartreuse-hued ones seem to go with almost every other color. The plants shouldn't require staking, especially if they have neighboring plants to lean on. The pleasant colors and appealing fragrance are always welcome!

GOOD CHOICES: the Nicki Series and Heaven Scent are excellent mixes; 'Lime Green' is the best greenish cultivar

Four O'-Clocks
Mirabilis jalapa
MATURE HEIGHT × WIDTH: 1-3 feet × 1-2 feet
FLOWER COLORS: magenta, pink, red, white, yellow
FLOWER SIZE: 2 inches
SOIL: moist, well drained

Also called marvel of Peru, this is a very tough plant of great beauty! It tolerates difficult conditions of drought, lousy soil, pollution, and relentless summer heat. Through it all, it keeps on blooming with lovely, trumpet-shaped flowers. The plant gets its name from the fact that the blooms really do open late in the day—they remain open through the evening and into the next day, when fresh ones replace them. They also bloom on overcast days. Hummingbirds love them. The color show is glorious; one plant may even display a variety of hues. Grow wherever you want plenty of bright, low-maintenance color. Be aware that they can reseed somewhat vigorously under the right conditions.

GOOD CHOICES: multicolored, splashy Kaleidoscope Mix; lower-growing Jingles Strain

Geranium
Pelargonium × hortorum
MATURE HEIGHT × WIDTH: 1-2 feet × 1-2 feet
FLOWER COLORS: red, orange, pink, mauve, white
FLOWER SIZE: 3-5 inch clusters
SOIL: moist, well drained

Perhaps you feel that geraniums are overused, especially the red ones. But look again: The newer varieties offer better-quality colors, denser flower clusters, attractively patterned leaves, and longer bloom periods. With a little creativity, you can combine them with other flowers to terrific effect. Nor do you have to confine them to containers or window boxes. Try tucking them into mixed beds or using a ribbon of similar-hued ones as an edging.

Geraniums are sure to look their best if you give them good, well-drained soil and a little attention from time to time. This means pinching them back for bushier, more compact growth, regular watering during dry spells, and snipping off blemished or dried-up leaves and flower clusters. In return, they will look fabulous.

GOOD CHOICES: 2002 AAS winner 'Black Velvet Rose' has pure pink flowers and nearly black leaves; burgundy-red 'Merlot'; pastel-hued Summer Showers Mix

ANNUALS AND BEDDING PLANTS

Impatiens
Impatiens walleriana
MATURE HEIGHT × **WIDTH:** 6 inches-2 feet × 1-2 feet
FLOWER COLORS: pink, salmon, lavender, white, red
FLOWER SIZE: 1-2 inches
SOIL: moist, well drained

For excellent color in shaded to partially shaded garden spots, impatiens is without peer. It's been around for a long time, and the newer varieties are clearly superior in terms of uniform flower color and flower size, not to mention a tidier growth habit. They're ideal in beds or along walkways, but also thrive in pots and planter boxes. For best results, make sure their soil doesn't dry out. Garden centers and seed companies offer a great range of hues every spring.

There are dozens of cultivars. Some are single-flowered and some are double. For broad areas mixes are great—either buy a mix already created or concoct your own from single-color flats. There are also tiny miniature forms, such as the hybrid Firefly Series. New Guinea impatiens (*Impatiens hawkeri*) is more tolerant of sun.

GOOD CHOICES: Blitz, Accent, Dazzler, and Super Elfin Series; 'Super Elfin Blue Pearl' is a luminous lavender

Lantana
Lantana camara
MATURE HEIGHT × **WIDTH:** 2-4 feet × 1-6 feet
FLOWER COLORS: pink, red, lilac, purple, pink, cream
FLOWER SIZE: 1-2 inch flower heads
SOIL: average, well drained

A substantial plant, almost like a small shrub, lantana takes up a fair amount of garden space if you allow it. However, if your plans are more modest—say you just want to dress up a planter box or hanging basket—lantana is very agreeable to grooming and pinching to keep it more compact. The flower heads are very bright and colorful, and keep on coming for practically the entire summer, particularly if you deadhead. The fragrance doesn't appeal to everyone (it's not at all sweet and a bit sharp), but butterflies and hummingbirds love the flowers. Lantana is reliably splendid in poor to average soil and bountiful sunshine.

GOOD CHOICES: 'Dallas Red' ('Texas Flame') has orange, yellow, and vivid red flowers; 'New Gold' has yellow flowers and is sterile (forms no seeds, thus needs no deadheading); 'Patriot Rainbow' is a hybrid with especially vivid multicolored blooms in red and yellow

Larkspur
Consolida ambigua (C. ajacis)
MATURE HEIGHT × WIDTH: 1-4 feet × 1 foot
FLOWER COLORS: blue, pink, white, bicolors
FLOWER SIZE: 1-2 inches
SOIL: well drained

Beloved for homegrown bouquets, larkspur is a relative of the more difficult-to-grow perennial delphinium. Its form is similar, that is, upright and often branched to display its bloom spikes like a candelabra, but its flowers are smaller, looser, and more casual. They perform best early in the season while the weather is still somewhat cool—summer heat and humidity finishes them off, alas. If the plants get tall, you can support them with twigs or let them lean on one another. It's fun to grow one of the mixes if you are planning to pick the flowers; they're fabulous fresh and also hold their color well when dried.

Larkspur makes a good filler plant in the garden with its ferny foliage and delicate spires of flowers, creating a romantic, cottage-garden effect. It can reseed, so if you pick regularly for bouquets, be sure to let a few plants go to seed so you can have them in the garden next year.

GOOD CHOICES: deep-colored 'Blue Cloud'; soft pink 'Earl Grey'; Kaleidoscope Mix; Dwarf Rocket Mix (no more than 2 feet tall)

Lobelia
Lobelia erinus
MATURE HEIGHT × WIDTH: 3-12 inches × 3-12 inches
FLOWER COLORS: blue, purple, red, white, bicolor
FLOWER SIZE: 1/2 inch
SOIL: moist, well drained

Blue is always a valuable color in the flower garden, and lobelia is a faithful source. The tiny tubular flowers are produced for months on end on small, trailing or cascading plants, carrying on even when neglected. They can get rangy and flower sparsely, however, if you forget to deadhead and do not keep their soil evenly moist. Try a skirt of the blue ones at the base of orange or yellow tuberous begonias. Or seek out less-common colors, such as brilliant cherry red. Lobelia fades in the heat of summer. Use as edging for a bed, or in containers.

GOOD CHOICES: 'Cambridge Blue' is the classic bright blue; 'Regatta Marine Blue' is blue-with-white-eye; 'Crystal Palace' has rich, dark blue blooms and bronzy-hued leaves; a good ruby red is 'Rosamond'

ANNUALS AND BEDDING PLANTS

Love-in-a-Mist
Nigella damascena
MATURE HEIGHT × WIDTH: 1-2 feet × 1 foot
FLOWER COLORS: blue, purple, rose, pink, white
FLOWER SIZE: 1-2 inches
SOIL: average, well drained

This is not a very widely grown flower, which is a shame. Love-in-a-mist delivers lots of good color over the summer months. The flowers get their common name from their unusual form, a combination of true petals, surrounding sepals, and a frilly ruff of green bracts. When they eventually fade away, ornamental balloon-like, striped seedpods follow, which are very popular with dried-flower arrangers and makers of wreaths.

The plants are easy to grow in full sun and average soil, and prosper in pots or in flower borders, where they weave their airy charms among the other flowers. Can reseed to the point of being a bit overwhelming, so let some go to seed in the garden, and harvest other flowers for fresh and dried arrangements.

GOOD CHOICES: Persian Jewels Series sports strong colors and tops out at 16 inches; 'Cramers' Plum' has brilliant white blossoms followed by plum-colored pods with no stripes

Marigold
Tagetes species and hybrids
MATURE HEIGHT × WIDTH: 6-18 inches × 12-18 inches
FLOWER COLORS: yellow, orange, white, maroon, red
FLOWER SIZE: 1-5 inches
SOIL: average, well drained

For bright and bold summer color, good old marigolds are hard to beat. They're also easy to grow and bloom often and well, which endears them to beginning gardeners. Others may find them "old hat," but one good way to gain fresh appreciation for the plants is to try offbeat or unexpected colors, such as cream or lemon yellow. Ribbon them through your perennial beds as edging or accent plants—you will be pleased with the results.

It's a good idea to make it a habit to deadhead spent marigold blooms. Also you can pinch back the plants every now and then to promote a bushier, more compact habit. And don't let their soil dry out, especially during very hot spells, or they'll throw in the towel.

GOOD CHOICES: 'Lemon Gem' signet marigold is a neat little plant with dainty, single-form flowers; Diamond Jubilee Mix has large, high-quality blooms

Melampodium
Melampodium species
MATURE HEIGHT × WIDTH: 8-12 inches × 8-12 inches
FLOWER COLORS: yellow, white
FLOWER SIZE: 1-2 inches
SOIL: average, well drained

Quite possibly one of the easiest daisies yet, melampodium is a relatively new find at the local nursery (and in need of a sporty, widely accepted common name!). It forms low, bushy mounds that are dense with handsome gray-green leaves and studded with little white (*Melampodium leucanthemum*) or golden (*M. paludosum*) flowers. The show goes on all summer long, with minimal assistance from you—once established, the plants are quite drought- and heat-tolerant. In mild climates, expect a year-round show, especially if you remember to keep the area watered. This is a great way to get lots of perky color for very little effort.

GOOD CHOICES: 'Derby' is a fine yellow that requires no deadheading; 'Medallion' is dark yellow

Million Bells
Calibrachoa hybrids
MATURE HEIGHT × WIDTH: 6-8 inches × 1-2 feet
FLOWER COLORS: violet, purple, pink, magenta, white
FLOWER SIZE: 1 inch
SOIL: moist, well drained

These look just like mini-petunias and, in fact, are closely related. No matter what you call them, these little beauties are incredibly floriferous. They remain in bloom all summer long, tolerating even periods of steamy weather or benign neglect. Their trailing habit makes them suitable for window boxes and all sorts of pots, but they are also wonderful weaving their glowing color in and among other, taller flowers in a mixed flowerbed. There is no need to deadhead, as is often the case with petunias. In warmer climates million bells can survive winter to bloom again the next year.

GOOD CHOICES: orange-red 'Terra Cotta', bright pink 'Coral Pink'

Nasturtium
Tropaeolum majus
MATURE HEIGHT × WIDTH: 8-15 inches × 12-15 inches
FLOWER COLORS: orange, yellow, red, white
FLOWER SIZE: 2-3 inches
SOIL: well drained

For abundant, bright color, you can't miss with nasturtiums. They grow eagerly, spread well without becoming a nuisance, and are always generous with their unique flowers. Traditionally orange or yellow, there are now crimson, cream-colored, and lemon-yellow forms, and varieties with variegated leaves for extra impact.

The plants have a pleasant peppery smell and all plant parts are completely edible. The leaves can be used in salads and the flowers are a pretty and tasty garnish. Even the seeds can be added to summer recipes (they taste a bit like capers).

Easy to grow from seed, nasturtium plants want only sunshine and regular water. Use them in pots, in hanging baskets, as an edging in the garden, tucked in at the feet of taller flowers; climbing and trailing ones can be trained to cascade down a rock wall or up over a trellis.

GOOD CHOICES: Alaska Mix has variegated leaves, with gold, orange, salmon, and mahogany flowers; Jewel Mix comes in hot colors; lovely 'Peach Melba' has a vanilla-white flower with maroon markings

Pansy
Viola × wittrockiana
MATURE HEIGHT × WIDTH: 6-9 inches × 6-9 inches
FLOWER COLORS: many
FLOWER SIZE: 2½-4 inches
SOIL: moist, well drained

Merry little blossoms, occasionally wafting a soft, sweet fragrance, abound on these utterly dependable old favorites. Some have a splash of contrasting yellow in the centers, some have markings called "whiskers" on their "faces." The hybridizers have thoroughly explored and expanded the color range, so you can now get a pansy in almost any hue you want. Some are dark and velvety, others are bright and bold, and still others are lovely pastel shades.

They look best in unified groupings (mix-and-match displays can look busy). Use in window boxes, pots, or tucked among larger flowers. They prefer some shade and extra water during very hot late spring days; they typically melt in the heat of summer. Violas are similar to pansies but have smaller flowers and a more compact form.

GOOD CHOICES: 'Imperial Antique Shades' is a lovely pastel mix of pink, lemon yellow, creamy white, and soft orange; 'Padparanja' has stunning, solid-color orange blossoms; Rhapsody Mix combines cherry-red flowers with white flowers with cherry-red centers—gorgeous!

Petunia
Petunia × *hybrida*
MATURE HEIGHT × **WIDTH:** 1 foot × 6 inches-3 feet
FLOWER COLORS: many
FLOWER SIZE: 2-4 inches
SOIL: moist, well drained

Although they've been around, and valued in the flower garden, for what seems like ages, petunias have enjoyed a recent flurry of attention and awards. For the larger, frilly flowered ones, the colors have improved (they're clearer and brighter), and the petals are tougher (much slower to wilt or fade). For the smaller-flowered, trailing ones, the Wave petunias have been a revolution, so productive, tough, and beautiful are they.

All petunias need good soil that drains well. Avoid placing them in exposed locations where hot sun blasts the life out of them and wind tatters them. But they are a better bet than ever for anyone seeking quick and easy color. Visit the garden center in early spring for the best array of choices, or check out the tantalizing selections in mail-order catalogs and order early.

GOOD CHOICES: 2004 AAS winner 'Limbo Violet', 2003 AAS winners 'Merlin Blue Morn' and 'Blue Wave', 2002 AAS winner 'Lavender Wave', 1994 AAS winner 'Purple Wave'

Portulaca
Portulaca grandiflora
MATURE HEIGHT × **WIDTH:** 6-8 inches × 8-12 inches
FLOWER COLORS: purple, red, hot pink, yellow, white
FLOWER SIZE: 1-2 inches
SOIL: average, well drained

Loads of bright little flowers adorn these naturally tough plants, which are able to withstand heat and drought with amazing resilience. Their ground-hugging habit helps, as do their moisture conserving, succulent needlelike leaves. Poor, dry, well-drained soil is ideal, and portulaca, or moss rose, will even thrive in rock gardens or gravelly areas. Several plants will carpet a broad area over time, reseeding and returning each year. Choose from an appealing array of flowers. Some are single and adorable in their own right; others are so double that they are fluffy with petals. The colors range from white and yellow to hot, lively shades of pink, red, and orange. Multi-colored displays are irresistible.

GOOD CHOICES: 'Giant Pink Radiance' has 3-inch blooms and loves to spill and tumble over walls or containers; Sundial Hybrid Mix has the full range of colors in double blossoms; Margarita Mix is similar but has a very dense growth habit (rosy pink 'Margarita Rosita' was a 2001 AAS winner)

Scarlet Sage
Salvia splendens
MATURE HEIGHT × WIDTH: 1-2 feet × 1-2 feet
FLOWER COLORS: red, purple, violet, white, pink
FLOWER SIZE: 1/2-2 inches
SOIL: moist, well drained

Snapdragon
Antirrhinum majus
MATURE HEIGHT × WIDTH: 1 1/2-3 feet × 1-3 feet
FLOWER COLORS: many
FLOWER SIZE: 1-2 inches
SOIL: moist, well drained

"Screeching red salvia," a fancy landscaper once wailed, "I can't bear to look at it!" But many gardeners continue to prize red salvias for their sparkling, dependable color—and hummingbirds and butterflies cannot resist them. Recent years have seen improved, less-muddy, longer-lasting reds, notably scarlet bold 'Flare', which look great with gray-leaved companions, such as dusty miller or artemisia.

But if red salvia is not for you, don't worry. There are many alternative colors, which retain the same valuable ability to keep blooming all summer in bedding displays, mixed beds, and even pots. 'Sangria' flowers are crisp white with red tips; 'Sea Breeze' is the same idea with lavender accents. Note that bicolor and pastel forms hold up better if they receive afternoon shade.

GOOD CHOICES: Salsa Series has very bright red flowers; Sizzler Series has a variety of bicolors; 'Sangria' is a white-and-red bicolor; 'Sea Breeze' is a lavender-and-white bicolor

If you want to grow your own bouquet flowers, snapdragons are a natural choice. They come in many bright and cheerful colors and bicolors, and grow quickly and easily. For best results, pinch them while still small (3 inches high or so) to encourage bushy growth and thus more flowers, and install slender twig or bamboo stakes to help support the show. You can get a second flush of bloom later in the summer if you harvest the first batch and follow up with water and fertilizer.

In the garden, snapdragons contribute their dense spikes of color to mixed flowerbeds. Tuck a few into a perennial border where other flowers are going in and out of bloom where you want some constant color to admire.

GOOD CHOICES: Liberty Mix sports the full range of colors on especially strong stems; sturdy Costa Mix features pastels, red, and white; Gum Drops Mix are dwarf plants, with 6-inch flower spikes and bicolors

Star-Cluster
Pentas lanceolata
MATURE HEIGHT × WIDTH: 1-2 feet × 1-2 feet
FLOWER COLORS: pink, red, purple, white
FLOWER SIZE: 3-4 inch clusters
SOIL: fertile, well drained

Technically a tender tropical shrubby plant, star-cluster (also called pentas and Egyptian star-cluster) performs beautifully in most of North America as an exuberant summertime annual, in the garden or in a pot. The crisp green foliage serves as a handsome backdrop for lots of perky flower clusters that give the plant its common name. Though usually available in mixes, you can sometimes get star-cluster in individual colors or white, which helps if you have a special garden color theme in mind. Butterflies and hummingbirds flock to the flowers.

Grow star-cluster in full sun, and remember to water and fertilize regularly so the plant will look its very best. If you snip the flowers to add to bouquets, you'll appreciate that they are especially long lasting.

GOOD CHOICES: Garden Sparkles Mix has dense clusters in the white-pink-red range; 'Star White' is the finest all-white one

Stock
Matthiola incana
MATURE HEIGHT × WIDTH: 6 inches-3 feet × 1 foot
FLOWER COLORS: red, purple, pink, white
FLOWER SIZE: 1 inch
SOIL: average, well drained

So long as your summers are not too hot, you will have no trouble growing gloriously fragrant stock. Some light shade is best in order to preserve flower color and scent; average soil that is neutral to slightly alkaline is ideal. In those conditions, this flower will grow quickly and easily and generate lots of blooms. The lush foliage is velvety and gray-green, a nice foil for the pastel flowers.

Plant plenty, so you can enjoy them in your garden, mixed with other bloomers, and still harvest some for bouquets. If you like to savor the scent, place a few containers of stock on your porch or deck; remember not to let their soil dry out.

GOOD CHOICES: Trysomic Mix has double flowers for extra impact, bred to be weather tough; the mostly double flowers of Giant Excelsior Mix have a non-branching habit that bouquet-pickers appreciate

ANNUALS AND BEDDING PLANTS

Sunflower
Helianthus annuus
MATURE HEIGHT × WIDTH: 1-15 feet × 1-3 feet
FLOWER COLORS: yellow, bronze, red, wine-red
FLOWER SIZE: 4-12 inches
SOIL: moist, well drained

No other flower can match sunflower for drama and fun in the summer garden. Hybridizers have had a field day with the species and there are many interesting choices, including ones that produce edible seeds for you or the birds, and sterile ones with smaller, fluffier flowers. The color range has been expanded well beyond plain old yellow to include bronze, red, wine-red, and bicolors. Grow a variety and harvest some of the easiest, most spectacular bouquets you've ever grown. The keys to sunflower success are lots of sunshine, adequate soil moisture (the bigger varieties are, understandably, more thirsty), and plenty of elbowroom. Some new varieties, developed especially for bouquets, also carry more numerous, smaller flowers on branching stems.

GOOD CHOICES: Inca Jewels Mix has strong stems that reach 5 to 8 feet high; 'Mammoth Giant' has huge, seed-laden flower heads; little 'Music Box', at 2 to 3 feet high, is a powerhouse of 4-inch blooms in yellow, gold, and bronze bicolors

Twinspur
Diascia barberae
MATURE HEIGHT × WIDTH: 6-10 inches × 12-20 inches
FLOWER COLORS: pink, rose, red
FLOWER SIZE: $1/2$-$3/4$ inch
SOIL: moist, well drained

Hailing from temperate sunny South Africa, twinspur is related to snapdragons, apparent in the tubular, lobed flowers. However, it is a lower-growing, mat-forming plant with slender, graceful stems bearing masses of the unique and beautiful blooms. Twinspur is most suitable for cottage-garden-style mixed beds, edgings, rock gardens, window boxes, and smaller pots. Especially hot summers are not good for the plants, but otherwise they are a cinch to grow well. All they ask is ample sunlight and fertile, well-drained, evenly moist soil to grow in. This is one of the newer annuals to hit the market, so you might have to search a bit to locate it, but it is definitely worth the effort.

GOOD CHOICES: 'Ruby Field' is widely acknowledged as the best bright pink; 'Blackthorn Apricot', from England, is a lovely, softer shade of apricot-pink

Verbena
Verbena × *hybrida*
MATURE HEIGHT × **WIDTH:** 1-2 feet × 1-2 feet
FLOWER COLORS: purple, red, white, pink, bicolors
FLOWER SIZE: 3-inch clusters
SOIL: average, well drained

A classic, heat-loving bedding plant, common verbena is very dependable. Some are low-growing mats, others are more upright. The foliage is generally a nice, neat green and the flower clusters—mostly in shades of purple and red, often with contrasting white eyes—are plentiful. Some have a sweet scent. Hummingbirds and butterflies are drawn to them. You can also clip the flowers to add to mixed bouquets; they hold their color and form quite well in a vase.

Verbena's sprawling form and abundant flowers recommend it for hanging baskets and pots, but it is equally valuable in the garden. Let it drape over a wall or enhance a rock garden, or plant several to fill in around taller flowers in a mixed bed. Growth will be bushier and more compact if you pinch it back occasionally. Water deeply and not too often.

GOOD CHOICES: 'Quartz Burgundy' was an AAS winner in 1999; 'Tickled Pink' is a nice clear pink; the Romance Series is a good mix

Zinnia
Zinnia elegans
MATURE HEIGHT × **WIDTH:** $1/2$-4 feet × $1/2$-2 feet
FLOWER COLORS: many
FLOWER SIZE: 1- to 5-inch flower heads
SOIL: moist, well drained

A great way to light up your garden! Zinnias come in all sorts of vivacious, hot colors, in an appealing range of flower forms (from almost daisy-like to plush, dahlia-like blooms to pom-poms). They mix very well with one another, in the garden or in a vase; they are one of the easiest and longest lasting bouquet flowers.

Full sun is all they demand. They are more flexible about soil, tolerating moderately damp to fairly dry. Older varieties are vulnerable to powdery mildew, which mars the leaves mid-season but doesn't affect the flower output. To avoid this problem, choose newer, resistant varieties and plant to allow good air circulation (that is, don't crowd them).

GOOD CHOICES: 'Profusion White' was an AAS winner in 2001; 'Profusion Orange' and 'Profusion Cherry' won in 1999; 'Envy' is a rarity, a cool green described as "the color of Granny Smith apples"; Benary's Giants Mix is outstanding for cut flowers, with rich colors and strong stems

Bulbs, Corms, and Tubers

all of these plants grow from an underground power source, whether it's a true bulb, rootstock, or thickened underground stem. Daffodils, tulips, and ornamental onions are true bulbs; crocus and gladiolus are corms; cannas and some types of begonias are tubers; most irises are rhizomes. These structures store the plant food that will generate stems, leaves, and of course flowers. A healthy, high-quality plant will have enough reserves to get it through at least one growing season, but most are perennial.

You are well advised to let the plants die down naturally. Bulb foliage tends to turn yellow, then brown and papery before fading away. If you intervene and cut away the unsightly leaves, you interrupt an important process: The fading leaves are sending food reserves down to the bulb, corm, or tuber below to provide for next year's show. If you can't bear to watch this process, you have two alternatives: Yank out the plants and treat them as annuals, replanting new ones each year, or "overplant" with something that will help hide the unattractive sight until the process is complete.

Beginning gardeners might have the impression that flowering bulbs, corms, and tubers are the province of the springtime garden. While it's true a lot of them do make an impressive show in the spring, others bloom in summer, and a few even flower in the fall. With some types of bulbs, such as tulips and daffodils, there is sufficient variation that you should be able to pull off a longer-blooming display if you plant several different species or named varieties, and early, midseason, and late bloomers. Confirm the exact bloom times when you buy (taking into account, of course, that every garden will have a slightly different result, depending not only on your location but on the weather).

Allium
Allium species
MATURE HEIGHT × WIDTH: 1-5 feet × 1 foot
FLOWER COLORS: purple, pink, white
FLOWER SIZE: 4-5 inch clusters
BLOOM TIME: summer to fall
SOIL: well drained
ZONES: 4-8

Ornamental onions are sun-lovers and prosper in well-drained soil. There are numerous species and forms, with a variety of flower-head sizes. Many have been bred to have very large flower heads, and stout stems to support them. They are best planted in groupings, with one another or with other tall flowers; shorter species can be tucked into the front of the bed. They also look showy in the company of clump-forming ornamental grasses. As cut flowers, they are excellent fresh or dried. Plant in the fall, when you are planting your tulips and daffodils. Spring will bring strappy leaves and, eventually, by early summer, the big flower show you've been looking forward to. *A. giganteum* is one of the most popular species, no doubt because it is so big and dramatic. *A. tuberosum* and *A. cernuum* have smaller but more numerous flower heads and bloom into fall.

GOOD CHOICES: 'White Giant' is an excellent white, as is the newer 'Mount Everest'; 'Globemaster' has enormous purple clusters, up to 10 inches around

Autumn Crocus
Colchicum autumnale
MATURE HEIGHT × WIDTH: 4-6 inches × 6-12 inches
FLOWER COLORS: lavender, rose, white
FLOWER SIZE: $1\frac{1}{2}$-3 inches
BLOOM TIME: mid-autumn
SOIL: average, well drained
ZONES: 4-8

Crocuses in the fall? Yes, it's true. Though technically not related to the springtime crocuses (they're in the lily family, while crocuses are in the iris family), they look similar, certainly in flower form—they are small, dainty, and have the same goblet shape. Their leaves are a little different; appearing in spring, they are long and lance-shaped.

The perky flowers come in shades of lavender, white, and rosy pink, a very welcome sight in the fall. You can plant colchicums in late summer, burying the little corms a few inches below the soil surface. Don't crowd them, because you need to allow room for the leaves. Because both foliage and flower are a bit informal, the best place to grow autumn crocuses is scattered among low perennials, or under trees.

GOOD CHOICES: 'Album' is a fine white; the white flowers of 'Alboplenum' are double, making them stand out dramatically in the fall; 'Pleniflorum' is a lilac-pink double

BULBS, CORMS, AND TUBERS

Buttercup
Ranunculus asiaticus

MATURE HEIGHT × WIDTH: 8-18 inches × 1-2 feet
FLOWER COLORS: yellow, orange, white, pink, red
FLOWER SIZE: 1-2 inches
BLOOM TIME: late spring to early summer
SOIL: fertile, well drained
ZONES: 8-11

You may have seen these at a florist and admired their plush, neat beauty and vivid colors. Good news: They're not hard to grow at home. Because they aren't very cold hardy, only gardeners in mild climates can put them in the ground in the fall. Everyone else can raise them in containers, or plant them in the spring and treat them as annuals. All they require is full sun and fertile soil that drains well. Don't water buttercups much until they start to poke their heads up above the soil, and then just give them regular soakings to encourage steady growth and plump flowers. When they appear in early summer, the blossoms are sensational: densely packed with silken petals and bursting with glorious color.

GOOD CHOICES: Tecolote Mixed is an excellent mixture; Turban Group Mix features double flowers that really stand out

Canna
Canna × *generalis*

MATURE HEIGHT × WIDTH: 5-6 feet × 1-2 feet
FLOWER COLORS: red, yellow, pink, bicolors
FLOWER SIZE: 4-6 inches
BLOOM TIME: midsummer to early fall
SOIL: fertile, moist, well drained
ZONES: 8-10

For many years, big, splashy cannas were consigned to the back of the flowerbed or the center of an island bed, with marigolds and red salvias strewn at their bases. But more recently "tropical gardening" has captured the imaginations of gardeners and landscapers throughout the country and suddenly cannas are getting a new lease on life. It helps that some of the newer cultivars are spectacular, such as 'Bengal Tiger' (also called 'Pretoria'), with its fiery orange flowers and variegated leaves of cream, gold, and green, and the lovely, award-winning 'Tropical Rose'. Exciting garden scenes can be created by adding showy canna plants into mixed flower borders (in pots, or in the ground as annuals). The leaf color, whether green, purple, or variegated, should also be considered when looking for companions.

GOOD CHOICES: Orange-flowered, variegated-leaved 'Bengal Tiger'; rosy-flowered 'Tropical Rose', a 1992 AAS winner; dwarf plants such as the Futurity and Pfitzer Series are suitable for containers

Crocus
Crocus vernus
MATURE HEIGHT × WIDTH: 4-5 inches × 3-4 inches
FLOWER COLORS: purple, white, yellow, bicolors
FLOWER SIZE: 1-2 inches
BLOOM TIME: early spring
SOIL: well drained
ZONES: 3-8

It's easy to grow Dutch crocus well. All you do is dig a small hole, drop in the flattened corm (if you can't tell which side is the top, plant them on edge), cover with soil, and water well unless autumn rains do it for you. Come spring, the show is sure to be terrific. Crocuses are ideal for early color in your flower beds, of course, but may also be added to rock gardens, along walkways, and even in small groups in your lawn. They're naturally vigorous plants and once they "get their legs under them," you'll find that they multiply, making a bigger and better springtime show in your yard every year.

GOOD CHOICES: rich purple 'Flower Record' is the best of its hue; glorious 'Pickwick' is lavender with purple stripes; 'Jeanne d'Arc' is a superb white; 'Yellow Mammoth' is a sunny yellow

Crown Imperial
Fritillaria imperialis
MATURE HEIGHT × WIDTH: 2-4 feet × 1-2 feet
FLOWER COLORS: orange, yellow, red
FLOWER SIZE: 2½ inches
BLOOM TIME: mid-spring
SOIL: moist, fertile, well drained
ZONES: 5-8

Despite what you might think when you first see its dramatic, unusual flowers and attention-grabbing color, crown imperial is not at all hard to grow. To get the best possible show, however, you need to plant the big, onion-size bulbs in late August in good, fertile soil and fairly deeply, 8 to 12 inches down. Come spring, a stout stem will emerge, soon decorated with leaves lower down and topped with a whorl of four to six bell-like, downward-facing flowers and a tuft of leaves above. This plant comes in hot colors, and the flowers also exude a pungent scent. Grow it with orange or yellow tulips and your spring garden will stop traffic.

GOOD CHOICES: the best, brightest orange is 'Rubra Maxima'; a nice, clear red is 'Aureomarginata' (so named because its leaves are gold-rimmed); 'Lutea' is an old favorite for yellow flowers

BULBS, CORMS, AND TUBERS

Daffodil
Narcissus species and hybrids
MATURE HEIGHT × WIDTH: 1-2 feet × 6-12 inches
FLOWER COLORS: white, yellow, orange, pink
FLOWER SIZE: 2-4 inches
BLOOM TIME: mid-spring
SOIL: well drained
ZONES: 3-8

There's good reason these spring bloomers are so enduringly popular. They're no trouble to plant or maintain, no pests nibble them, they increase their numbers every year, and they come in a nice array of forms and colors. Plant about 6 inches deep and apart in full or partial sun. An application of bulb food (follow the directions on the label) every spring will encourage more blooms the following year.

Recent years have seen a flurry of new daffodils. These have more durable flowers that stand up to variable spring weather and last longer in a vase. Gardeners are also rediscovering the charms of the old-fashioned, smaller-flowered, sweet-scented daffodils.

GOOD CHOICES: the classic 'Dutch Master' still sets the standard (though many labeled as such are not the true variety); 'Ice Follies' is soft white and lemon yellow; of the pink-cupped ones, 'Easter Bonnet' is impressive; multi-stemmed, small-flowered 'Thalia' is deliciously fragrant; perky, 'Tête-à-Tête' has petite yellow-on-yellow blooms

Dahlia
Dahlia hybrids
MATURE HEIGHT × WIDTH: 2-5 feet × 1-2 feet
FLOWER COLORS: many
FLOWER SIZE: 3-12 inches
BLOOM TIME: late summer and fall
SOIL: moist, well drained
ZONES: 7-10

Few other flowers can rival dahlias for sensational presence or color in the late summer and fall—just when your garden needs it most. If you do not live in a mild climate, you can either treat dahlias as annuals or dig them up and store them indoors for the winter months. The time to plant the husky tuberous roots is in spring, after all danger of frost is past. Give them a sunny spot in fertile, well-drained soil that is damp or kept well watered (but don't over-water, because they hate "wet feet"). Don't fertilize much, either, or you'll get more foliage than flowers. Well-stocked nurseries always offer a nice array of colors and flower sizes to choose from, but if you really want to have fun with your dahlia displays, shop from the swoon-worthy selections in the mail-order catalogs of dahlia or bulb specialists.

GOOD CHOICES: huge, glowing yellow flowers adorn 'Kelvin's Floodlight'; for true orange, try 'Mrs. Eileen'; for true red, 'Barbarossa'

Gladiola
Gladiolus hybrids
MATURE HEIGHT × WIDTH: 3-4 feet × 6 inches
FLOWER COLORS: many
FLOWER SIZE: 2-4 inches
BLOOM TIME: summer
SOIL: well drained
ZONES: 7-10

Few other flowers come in such an amazing array of colors. There are also numerous dwarf varieties with proportionally smaller leaves and flower spikes. You can make a pastel-themed display, or concentrate on hot colors.

Because glads are so tall and distinctive, they don't always fit in easily with other flowers. Instead, it's best to plant them out in long rows, sometimes with support for the tall ones. (A good trick is to plant the corms extra-deep, 6 to 8 inches down, to anchor them better in the ground; otherwise, a strong wind may topple them.) If you stagger the plantings every two weeks or so, you'll harvest armloads of bouquets all summer long. Note that the best time to pick glads is when the first few flowers at the base of the spike are completely open.

GOOD CHOICES: 'Shocking' has pristine-white petals centered with ruby red; 'Blues' is soft white suffused with lilac; intriguing 'Green Star' is silky lime-green; 'Nova Lux' is an outstanding golden yellow

Glory-of-the-Snow
Chionodoxa luciliae
MATURE HEIGHT × WIDTH: 4-6 inches × 4-6 inches
FLOWER COLORS: blue, pink, white, bicolors
FLOWER SIZE: 1/2-1 inch
BLOOM TIME: early spring
SOIL: average, well drained
ZONES: 3-9

Though it got its evocative name from the fact that it appears just as the snow is melting in its native Greek mountains, glory-of-the-snow usually bursts on the scene a little later in the spring in this country. It's a fall-planted bulb, like tulips and daffodils, but smaller and not as dramatic. As such, your best bet is to plant lots of them. The electric-blue, white-eyed blossoms look fabulous in drifts under trees and shrubs, and naturally increase their numbers from one year to the next. Like other spring-blooming bulbs, you should let the foliage die down naturally so it can convey food to the bulb for next year's show. Luckily, glory-of-the-snow is small and doesn't call attention to itself as it fades away.

GOOD CHOICES: the species is bright blue; 'Alba' is a white cultivar; larger 'Pink Giant' is available from some specialty bulb catalogs

BULBS, CORMS, AND TUBERS

Grape Hyacinth
Muscari species
MATURE HEIGHT × WIDTH: 4-8 inches × 4-8 inches
FLOWER COLORS: blue, white, bicolors
FLOWER SIZE: 1-3 inch spikes
BLOOM TIME: mid-spring
SOIL: fertile, well drained
ZONES: 4-8

There's no easier or more pleasant way to landscape under deciduous trees than to plant ribbons and drifts of grape hyacinth. They will spread out over the years, so use them for color in a more carefree, casual area of your yard. The classic species is deep blue, but if you search around at good nurseries and in mail-order catalogs, you might enjoy some of the newly available alternatives, including all-white ones and blue-and-white bicolors.

Plant the small bulbs in early autumn, about twice as deep as the size of the bulb. Foliage will likely appear, but that is normal. The spring show will be on track after winter comes and goes. There's no need to fertilize or fuss over them—grape hyacinths are truly carefree flowers.

GOOD CHOICES: 'Cantab' has double blue flowers and sweet fragrance for extra impact; 'Album' is a good white; beautiful, unusual 'Mount Hood' has white-topped cobalt-blue spikes; 'Valerie Finnis' has pale blue flowers

Hyacinth
Hyacinthus orientalis
MATURE HEIGHT × WIDTH: 8-12 inches × 8-12 inches
FLOWER COLORS: purple, blue, pink, white, red, yellow
FLOWER SIZE: 8-12 inch spikes
BLOOM TIME: spring
SOIL: moist, well drained
ZONES: 5-9

While other spring bulbs seem best suited to informal planting schemes, hyacinths look much better when put into a more formal plan. This is because their dense flower spikes are so neat and uniform. So plant them (in the fall, of course) about 8 inches or so deep and fairly close together for best results. Grow a mix in small groupings, or invest in single colors and ribbon them through your spring displays. As they start to burgeon in the spring, check on the double ones and stake them if necessary, as they can become a bit top-heavy. All hyacinths are richly scented, a happy sign that spring has arrived in your garden. Typically used as a one-shot annual, some hyacinths will come back for several years.

GOOD CHOICES: plush, taller (to 10 inches) white flowers grace 'Carnegie'; 'Woodstock' is plum purple; some specialty catalogs carry the rare but lovely yellow 'City of Haarlem'

Lily
Lilium species and hybrids
MATURE HEIGHT × WIDTH: 2-7 feet × 1-2 feet
FLOWER COLORS: many
FLOWER SIZE: 4-10 inches
BLOOM TIME: summer
SOIL: moist, well drained
ZONES: 5-9

Gorgeous lilies are actually not difficult at all to grow. With a little planning, you can have lilies in bloom in your yard from early summer till fall. Include the smaller-flowered (4 to 6 inch) but vivid-hued Asiatic lilies, the trumpets, and the big, scented Oriental lilies (with blooms 6 to 10 inches or more across!). Species lilies typically have smaller flowers, arranged in tiers; most bloom in the latter part of the summer.

Plant lilies in the fall or as soon as possible in spring. Don't crowd them; they look better and are healthier if they have some air circulation—a foot apart is ideal. Note that the plants are slow to emerge, but don't give up on them—they'll appear in late spring and soon make up for lost time.

GOOD CHOICES: golden yellow 'Connecticut King' is a justly popular Asiatic; two-toned pink 'Montreaux' is another Asiatic beauty; Aurelian Hybrids are excellent trumpets; pristine white, deliciously scented 'Casablanca' is the classic white Oriental; Martagon, or Turk's cap, lilies are tall with nodding flowers, some with recurved petals

Lycoris
Lycoris species
MATURE HEIGHT × WIDTH: 18-30 inches × 1-2 feet
FLOWER COLORS: pink, red
FLOWER SIZE: 2-4 inches
BLOOM TIME: late summer and fall
SOIL: moist, well drained
ZONES: *L. squamigera*, 6-10; *L. radiata*, 8-10

For late-season color, these lily relatives are fantastic. Tall, fleshy stems emerge first and show off the most amazing blooms, complete with reflexed or wavy-edged spidery petals (technically "tepals") and prominent stamens. The flowers of *Lycoris squamigera* are pink, trumpet shaped, fragrant, and carried in dramatic groups of up to eight; those of *L. radiata* are red or deep pink, spidery in form, and carried in groups of up to six. The strap-shaped leaves appear later.

If you grow them in the ground, give lycoris good, rich soil; even moisture; and some companions, both to mark the spot (when the lilies are not evident) and to flatter the flowers, such as ferns, hostas, and colorful annuals. In pots, don't plant too deeply and don't neglect watering.

GOOD CHOICES: only the species described above are widely available

Snowdrops
Galanthus nivalis
MATURE HEIGHT × WIDTH: 1 foot × 1 foot
FLOWER COLORS: white
FLOWER SIZE: $1/2$-$3/4$ inch
BLOOM TIME: early spring
SOIL: rich, moist, well-drained
ZONES: 3-9

How aptly named this charming bulb is! Crisp little pendant-shaped flowers burst forth just as the snow is melting in cool climates, bringing cheer to any gardener who ventures outdoors early in the season. The flowers are snowy white, tipped and banded with green, which actually helps them stand out more. There's only one flower per arching stem, but the stems can be numerous on a clump, emerging from tufts of grassy leaves. And snowdrops are eager "naturalizers," meaning that a handful of plants can expand to become a substantial colony over the years. Your display will be safe because their bulbs are distasteful to rodents and deer.

Plant snowdrops at the base of deciduous shrubs or trees, in good, humusy soil and partial shade. Here, they will thrive and never fail to delight you every spring.

GOOD CHOICES: the species is lovely in its own right; 'Flore Pleno' has double flowers; 'Sam Arnott' has large flowers; for more impact, try the taller "giant" snowdrop, *Galathus elwesii*, which also blooms up to two weeks earlier

Tulip
Tulipa species and hybrids
MATURE HEIGHT × WIDTH: 6-18 inches × 4-8 inches
FLOWER COLORS: many
FLOWER SIZE: 2-6 inches
BLOOM TIME: spring
SOIL: fertile, well drained
ZONES: 3-8

There are countless gorgeous individual varieties and species of tulips to try and, with a little forethought in the fall, you can plan for spectacular color-themed displays that start in early spring and continue almost up to the edge of summer.

A sunny spot with good, fertile soil is always important, but just as important is proper drainage. Tulips are miserable in low places and soggy ground and should not be over-watered. Plant the bulbs in the fall, pointed end up, about three times as deep as they are tall. Don't worry—they'll work their way to the surface by spring. If you have deer or squirrels in the neighborhood, you may have to take protective measures—ask for advice at your local nursery.

GOOD CHOICES: 'Angelique' is a peach-pink peony-flowered favorite; a very dramatic, classic Triumph type is purple 'Attila'; crimson, strong-stemmed "single late" 'Kingsblood' is stunning; another is wine-red 'Queen of the Night'; the cultivars of *Tulipa greggii* are shorter-stemmed and offer splendid, vivid colors

Windflower
Anemone blanda
MATURE HEIGHT × WIDTH: 6-8 inches × 6-8 inches
FLOWER COLORS: purple, pink, white
FLOWER SIZE: 2 inches
BLOOM TIME: early spring
SOIL: well drained
ZONES: 4-8

Dainty, daisy-like flowers for early spring? It sounds like a novelty, but it's true—and windflowers couldn't be easier to grow. They are more of a groundcover, so growing a mix makes a wonderfully appealing carpet of early color. Buy the bulbs in quantity in the fall and strew them informally under trees or around shrubs in your yard, planting them about 5 inches down (with these bulbs, it's impossible to tell which end is up, so plant them sideways and they'll be fine). Mulch if your winters are chilly, and wait for spring. They will appear about the same time as daffodils and, indeed, the two look very pretty together.

GOOD CHOICES: usually sold as a mix of white, pink, and purple; oddly named 'Radar' is rosy pink with white centers; 'White Splendour' makes a great carpet for mixed tulip beds

Winter Aconite
Eranthis hyemalis
MATURE HEIGHT × WIDTH: 3-4 inches × 3-4 inches
FLOWER COLORS: yellow
FLOWER SIZE: $3/4$-$1^1/2$ inches
BLOOM TIME: late winter to early spring
ZONES: 4-6
SOIL: moist, well drained

Like other spring bloomers, these lovelies thrive on late-winter and early spring sunshine, such as at the edge of trees or shrubs, and don't mind shade later in the season when their flowering period is over and they are about to go dormant. They are prized because they appear so very early in the season and their abundant, cheery little yellow flowers are such a bright sight after a long, cold winter. Because they are petite, it's best to plant a grouping, at the front of the bed. Over the years, they'll self-sow and spread, making a bigger and bigger carpet of color that you can look forward to every year. The tubers are small; they resemble small dried-up sticks. But if you soak them in water the night before you plant them (in the fall, with your other spring bulbs), they'll plump up. Set them an inch or two deep and don't worry about which end is up.

GOOD CHOICES: while there are no cultivars of this species, a closely related species is *Eranthis cilicica*

Perennials
and Biennials

If you've had a routine of planting plentiful annuals every spring and summer and are starting to think that all that money and planting is getting to be too much, you are ready for perennials. Perennials return to grow and rebloom every year in your garden, meaning you only have to plant them once. Best of all, many perennials obligingly grow bigger and better with each passing year, settling into your garden and producing lots of flowers.

However, a wag once defined a perennial as "a plant that, had it lived, would've bloomed again." If you don't want to experience the frustration and disappointment, not to mention the expense, of perennials that end up acting like annuals, you need to start by choosing plants wisely. Learn what perennials thrive in your climate. Then learn what growing conditions various perennials need to succeed and place the right plant in the right site. For more information and help with this, consult Chapter 2.

The following perennials are good ones, plants that have been proven to perform well in the generally average conditions that most of us have in our yards. Note that there are two types of good perennials: old favorites and outstanding newcomers. Old favorites are still in commerce simply because they've stood the test of time, and you can plant them with confidence. As for the newcomers, because plant breeders are dedicated to selecting the best performers from among hundreds and thousands, a fresh introduction is frequently also a safe bet. The plants listed here will not all work well in all parts of the country, so be attentive to your particular location.

Aster
Aster species and hybrids
MATURE HEIGHT × WIDTH: 1-6 feet × 2-4 feet
FLOWER COLORS: white, pink, lavender, purple, red
FLOWER SIZE: 1-3 inches
BLOOM TIME: late summer to fall
SOIL: well drained
ZONES: 4-8

This is a great group of late-season bloomers, indispensable at a time of year when your garden can use a burst of color. Bushy and sturdy, the wild forms of asters are studded with small daisies of white, pale blue, or pink, but hybridizers have introduced new hues and colors. Ironically, these native American plants have received the most attention overseas, particularly from English and German plant breeders . Now the flowers are much bigger and the colors are more vivid. There are rosy pinks and rich purples, wonderful on their own in the autumn garden or planted together.

Tuck shorter plants in front of your asters to hide their lower stems and expand the display, or pinch the asters back several times before midsummer to encourage bushiness.

GOOD CHOICES: cultivars of *A. novae-angliae*, the New England aster, are hot pink 'Alma Potschke', pastel pink 'Harrington's Pink', and 'Mt. Everest' with spectacular large, double, white flowers

Astilbe
Astilbe species and hybrids
MATURE HEIGHT × WIDTH: $1^{1}/_{2}$-4 feet × $1^{1}/_{2}$-$2^{1}/_{2}$ feet
FLOWER COLORS: white, pink, lavender, red
FLOWER SIZE: 6-12 inch clusters
BLOOM TIME: spring and summer
SOIL: fertile, moist, well drained
ZONES: 3-8

Among the most beautiful of all shade perennials, astilbes are easy to grow in moist, fertile ground. They return in glory every year, and are rarely ever troubled by pests or diseases. The magnificent feathery plumes—actually masses of tiny flowers—come in a range of colors, from white to lavender to pink to red. Bloom times vary, so if you plan carefully, you can enjoy a long period of color in your shade garden. After the blooms finally fade, the somewhat ferny, toothed leaflets look handsome for the rest of the season. Popular ways to use this fine plant include in a formal bed in the shade of a tree; in a sweep in a woodland area; or along the banks of a pool, pond, or stream.

GOOD CHOICES: light pink 'Sprite' was a PPA winner in 1994

Baby's Breath

Gypsophila paniculata

MATURE HEIGHT × WIDTH: 1-4 feet × 3-4 feet
FLOWER COLORS: white, pink
FLOWER SIZE: 3/8 inch
BLOOM TIME: early to midsummer
SOIL: neutral to slightly alkaline, moist
ZONES: 3-7

Though many people think of baby's breath as a florist's plant, there's nothing tricky about growing your own. The plant takes up a fair amount of space, however, almost like a small shrub, so be sure to give it enough room to spread out. When happy—given plenty of sun, regular water, and fertile soil that is a bit on the alkaline side—the plant will grow robustly and cover itself in sprays of adorable little flowers. You can snip off stems for fresh bouquets or let them dry for use in dried arrangements or wreath making. The plants are so prolific that you'll always have plenty of blooms.

GOOD CHOICES: double-flowered white 'Bristol Fairy', double-flowered 'Pink Fairy'

Balloon Flower

Platycodon grandiflorus

MATURE HEIGHT × WIDTH: 1 1/2-2 1/2 feet × 1 foot
FLOWER COLORS: blue, white, pink
FLOWER SIZE: 2 inches
BLOOM TIME: summer
SOIL: average, well drained
ZONES: 3-9

In the bud stage, the flowers of this bellflower relative are shaped like small balloons. On any given plant, on any given summer day, there are flowers on a plant in both stages—it's a conversation piece, to be sure, but balloon flower is also simply a good, dependable plant to have in your flower garden. It comes in blue, pink, and white, and looks quite fetching if you plant several plants of different colors together. It also makes a long-lasting cut flower. As for culture, it's easy. Balloon flower loves full sun but adapts to shade. It does fine in most soils, provided they're neither too wet nor too dry. Diseases and pests never bother it. In short, it's a great plant. If you routinely deadhead spent flowers, it will continue to bloom most of the summer.

GOOD CHOICES: 'Fuji' is a good mix, worth growing if you're planning to pick bouquets; 'Hakone Blue' has double blue flowers with some white veining; 'Fairy Snow' has big flowers on a shorter, 10-inch plant; 'Fuji Pink' is pale pink

Bearded Iris
Iris hybrids
MATURE HEIGHT × WIDTH: 3-4 feet × 2-3 feet
FLOWER COLORS: many
FLOWER SIZE: 4-7 inches
BLOOM TIME: late spring to early summer
SOIL: fertile, well drained
ZONES: 4-9

For color range alone, the bearded irises are fantastic. If all you've ever seen or grown are the pale purple or yellow ones, take another look at the tantalizing array of choices. The real bonanza—and your best bet—is in the retail catalogs of mail-order specialists, who are often also the iris breeders. Here you will find soft candied pink, tangerine orange, sky blue, and peach. Some are even fragrant, and some rebloom later in the year and are called "remontant" irises.

Bearded irises are uniquely suited to bicolor combinations because they are in two parts—with the top, erect petals called "standards," and lower, downward-swooping petals called "falls." The top industry award is called the Dykes Medal; winners of this are a good place to start.

GOOD CHOICES: look for 1982 Dykes Medal winner coral pink 'Beverly Sills'; 1993 winner, bicolor yellow-and-lavender 'Edith Wolford' is equally lovely

Bee Balm
Monarda didyma
MATURE HEIGHT × WIDTH: 2-4 feet × 1-2 feet
FLOWER COLORS: red, white, pink, lavender
FLOWER SIZE: 2-4 inches
BLOOM TIME: mid- to late summer
SOIL: moist, well drained
ZONES: 4-8

Splashy flowers adorn tall, handsome plants clothed in mint-green foliage. Horticulturists have lavished attention on this fine perennial, resulting in beautiful, bigger-flowered selections in shades from ruby red to wine purple to pure white to soft pink. Improved foliage has also been a focus, because this plant's leaves are vulnerable to powdery mildew. Adequate spacing at planting time (set plants several feet apart) allows for air circulation, but choosing a cultivar expressly labeled "mildew resistant" is also wise.

In full sun and moisture-retentive soil (don't forget to mulch), bee balms are sensational for many long weeks every summer. As a bonus, the flowers also draw the attention of butterflies and hummingbirds!

GOOD CHOICES: 'Gardenview Scarlet', dark red 'Jacob Cline', pink 'Marshall's Delight', maroon 'On Parade' (all billed as mildew resistant)

Bellflower
Campanula species
MATURE HEIGHT × WIDTH: 1-3 feet × 1-3 feet
FLOWER COLORS: blue, purple, pink, white
FLOWER SIZE: 2-3 inches
BLOOM TIME: late spring to summer
SOIL: well drained
ZONES: 3-8

The time between late spring's bulbs and midsummer's perennials is sometimes a difficult gap to fill in the flower garden. Bellflowers to the rescue! They are attractive, easy to grow, and come in a broad variety of plant habits to suit all sorts of situations. Taller ones such as *C. latifolia* and *C. persicifolia* can display their pretty bells in the back of a border or along a fence or wall. Lower-growing ones such as *C. carpatica*, *C. poscharskyana*, and *C. portenschlagiana* are suited for the middle or front of a border, an embankment, or even planter boxes and pots. Well-drained soil of average fertility is fine for all of these.

Flower colors for bellflowers are generally in the blue, lavender, and pink range, plus pure white. Keep the show going by picking bouquets and deadheading.

GOOD CHOICES: *C. carpatica* 'Blue Clips' and 'White Clips' are outstanding, heavy bloomers; *C. persicifolia* comes in various shades of purple as well as white, China blue 'Telham Beauty' being the finest

Black-Eyed Susan
Rudbeckia species
MATURE HEIGHT × WIDTH: 2-3 feet × 2-3 feet
FLOWER COLORS: yellow
FLOWER SIZE: 3-5 inches
BLOOM TIME: midsummer to fall
SOIL: average, well drained
ZONES: 3-8

Brilliant black-eyed Susans are among the easiest and longest lasting of all garden perennials, producing armloads of bright flowers for a minimum of effort on your part. No summer garden should be without them. They also make excellent, long-lasting cut flowers and even hold their bright color when dried.

The best one is widely acknowledged to be tall, prolific *R. fulgida* var. *sullivantii* 'Goldsturm', but softer-yellow ones are available. And recent years have seen a flurry of fast-growing black-eyed Susans that are often treated like annuals, mostly selections of *R. hirta*. All like average, well-drained soil and benefit from soil moisture.

GOOD CHOICES: superb 4-inch flowers adorn 'Goldsturm', the 1999 PPA winner; *R. hirta* 'Indian Summer' is a yellow-and-maroon bicolor and won an AAS award in 1995; the 2003 AAS winner, 'Prairie Sun', is a yellow-and-gold bicolor with green centers

Blanket Flower
Gaillardia × *grandiflora*
MATURE HEIGHT × WIDTH: 2-3 feet × 1-2 feet
FLOWER COLORS: red and yellow
FLOWER SIZE: 3-4 inches
BLOOM TIME: summer
SOIL: average, well drained
ZONES: 3-8

A natural for low-maintenance gardens, blanket flower blooms with especially bright, vibrant hues—usually bold red fringed in yellow. It's an easy-going plant, tolerating average soil, benign neglect, and long, hot summers. Very adaptable, it looks fabulous with any other yellow daisy, from black-eyed Susan to coreopsis, as well as blue spiky bloomers like salvia and veronica.

Because it is a clump-former, and a reasonably tidy one at that, blanket flower also does well as a tall edging plant, in planter boxes, or in decorative pots displayed on a sunny patio or deck. The somewhat fuzzy green foliage is pest and disease free, and deer don't nibble the plants.

GOOD CHOICES: splashy 'Fanfare' has quilled petals and is astoundingly prolific; 2003 AAS winner vivid 'Sundance Bicolor'; dwarf 'Goblin' only reaches 8 to 12 inches; for a solid-color alternative, try beautiful wine-red 'Burgundy' or 1991 AAS winner 'Red Plume'

Blazing Star
Liatris spicata
MATURE HEIGHT × WIDTH: 2-3 feet × 1 foot
FLOWER COLORS: white, pink, lavender, magenta
FLOWER SIZE: 12-15 inch spikes
BLOOM TIME: summer
SOIL: fertile, well drained
ZONES: 3-9

As tough as it is beautiful, blazing star has a lot going for it. Because the species comes from the American prairies, it likes to be grown in full sun, doesn't mind average soil (so long as it's well-drained—soggy ground is fatal), and is admirably drought tolerant. The species form has been greatly improved to have flowers that are denser and longer lasting. The color range has also been extended to include lighter purple and white. Indeed, so outstanding are the flower spikes that they are favorites of flower arrangers and florists. There's no reason you can't grow your own for bouquets! Just plant plenty, because they also fit very well into sunny borders...and butterflies adore them.

GOOD CHOICES: florist-quality blooms can be found on 'Floristan Violet' and 'Floristan White'; a shorter (15-inch), lavender edition is 'Kobold'

PERENNIALS AND BIENNIALS

Bleeding Heart
Dicentra spectabilis

MATURE HEIGHT × WIDTH: 2-3 feet × 2 feet
FLOWER COLORS: white, pink
FLOWER SIZE: 1 inch
BLOOM TIME: spring
SOIL: well drained
ZONES: 2-8

A wonderfully long-blooming plant, bleeding heart is a great way to bring color to a shady area. With little fuss, it bursts forth reliably every spring and lines its arching stems with adorable locket-shaped flowers. These remain on the plant for up to six weeks! The handsome, loose, ferny foliage lingers for several weeks after blooming is finished, but then begins to fade away and go dormant. Still, for a period in late spring and early summer, bleeding heart is the star. Two native species, *D. eximia* (eastern U.S.) and *D. formosa* (western U.S.) have a low, mounding form and smaller pink flowers.

GOOD CHOICES: the species, which is pink flowered, is outstanding; 'Alba' is the white version

Boltonia
Boltonia asteroides

MATURE HEIGHT × WIDTH: 4-6 feet × 2-4 feet
FLOWER COLORS: white, pink
FLOWER SIZE: 3/4-1 inch
BLOOM TIME: late summer to mid-fall
SOIL: fertile, moist, well drained
ZONES: 4-9

Covered with countless small white daisies late every summer and fall, boltonia is an outstanding long-blooming perennial for that time of year. The white flowers seem to glow in the evening hours. The plant can get fairly big and floppy, so it needs careful placement (to give it enough room) and perhaps staking as well. You can plant it next to another big fall-bloomer such as Russian sage or an aster, and let them lean into one another. Or try the cultivar 'Snowbank', which is more compact.

Moist, organically rich soil is important for boltonia's success. Fall rains might provide the necessary supplemental water, or you can put down a moisture-conserving mulch. Unlike its cousins, the asters, it does not get leggy and is not susceptible to mildew.

GOOD CHOICES: the popular 'Snowbank' is more compact than the species; also compact, but with pretty pink daisies, is 'Pink Beauty'; dwarf 'Nana' has pinkish-lilac flowers and only reaches 24 to 28 inches

Cardinal Flower
Lobelia cardinalis
MATURE HEIGHT × WIDTH: 3-5 feet × 1 foot
FLOWER COLORS: red, white, pink
FLOWER SIZE: 1-1¹/₂ inches
BLOOM TIME: summer
SOIL: moist, well drained
ZONES: 3-8

A wildflower found in damp meadows and along streams in nature, it transitions easily to garden life, so long as its moisture requirement is fulfilled. The fact that the fan-shaped flowers can vary from the usual bright red (which is terrific in its own right). You can now grow forms that are magenta, hot pink, royal purple, soft pink, and white. As a bonus, hummingbirds are sure to come flitting by.

Note that the flowers last longer and the color is better when the plants are grown in partial shade. Cardinal flower also makes a wonderful cut flower; its slender stems and graceful beauty make nice filler in bouquets, particularly with other flowers that bloom in spires, but also with white or pink roses.

GOOD CHOICES: 'Ruby Slippers' has dark, velvety, ruby-red blooms; those of 'Heather Pink' are pastel pink; 'Monet Moment' is darker pink; 'Alba' is a good white; spectacular 'Queen Victoria' is a hybrid with dark, bronzy leaves to contrast with its scarlet flowers

Columbine
Aquilegia species and hybrids
MATURE HEIGHT × WIDTH: 2-3 feet × 1-2 feet
FLOWER COLORS: many
FLOWER SIZE: 2-4 inches
BLOOM TIME: late spring to early summer
SOIL: moist, well drained
ZONES: 3-9

Jaunty, multicolored flowers drift above charming, ferny leaves late every spring and into the first weeks of summer. Columbines are not only bright and pretty, they're also very easy. They do best in full sun and well-drained soil; if the soil is not naturally moist, just water regularly to encourage the best possible flower show.

Pests, diseases, deer, and rodents do not bother them. The only possible problem is a tiny insect called a leaf miner that creates a tracery pattern on the leaves; just cut off affected parts and the plant will generate fresh foliage.

GOOD CHOICES: McKana Giants Mix is the best if you want a full range of colors and bicolors with large flowers; the Biedermeier Strain features white, pinks, and purples; 'Maxistar' is all yellow; unusual 'Nora Barlow' has fluffy double flowers of pink and mauve

Coneflower
Echinacea purpurea
MATURE HEIGHT × WIDTH: 2-4 feet × 1-2 feet
FLOWER COLORS: purple, pink, white, orange
FLOWER SIZE: 3-4 inches
BLOOM TIME: summer
SOIL: well drained
ZONES: 3-9

Not long after gardeners welcomed this superior, long-lasting daisy into their gardens, hybridizers began to capitalize on it. It has handsome, disease-free foliage and strong stems that don't need staking, plus it's hardy, widely adaptable, and drought-tolerant. Coneflower also looks great in mixed flower borders, contributing plentiful, long-term, carefree color. It makes a fine bouquet flower, fresh or dried.

The flower of the species is shuttlecock-shaped with purple petals (ray flowers) and a prominent, orange-tinged cone (disk flowers) that butterflies alight on. A bigger-flowered variety whose rosy-pink petals are straighter, 'Magnus', won the PPA award in 1998. Now there's orange-petaled 'Meadowbrite', and a novel bright pink one with a boss of extra petals in the center called 'Razzmatazz'.

GOOD CHOICES: 'Magnus' was the PPA winner in 1998; orange 'Meadowbrite'™; double pink 'Razzmatazz'; green-tinged white 'Kim's Mophead'; compact-growing 'Kim's Knee-High'

Coreopsis
Coreopsis species
MATURE HEIGHT × WIDTH: 1-3 feet × 2-3 feet
FLOWER COLORS: yellow, pink, wine-red
FLOWER SIZE: 1-3 inches
BLOOM TIME: summer
SOIL: well drained
ZONES: 5-9

Free-flowering coreopsis is the perfect plant for a busy person. All you have to do is give it a sunny spot; it tolerates infertile or dry soil and sails through hot summers with little attention or care. A rather loose, open growth habit and fine-textured foliage help coreopsis fit into mixed flowerbeds well, where it can weave among other perennials or annuals.

The superb *C. verticillata* 'Moonbeam', with small daisies of soft lemon yellow, is probably the most versatile, happy in the company of practically every other flower color. Some of the brighter yellow ones are best with other bold colors (red, purple, blue), particularly the double-flowered forms because they stand out.

GOOD CHOICES: 'Moonbeam' was the PPA winner in 1992; dwarf 'Zagreb' reaches only 8 to 10 inches; 'Sweet Dreams' shows off white flowers blending to hot pink toward the center; fluffy flowered, golden *C. grandiflora* 'Early Sunrise' won an AAS award in 1989

Crocosmia
Crocosmia hybrids
MATURE HEIGHT × WIDTH: 2-3 feet × 1-2 feet
FLOWER COLORS: yellow, orange, red
FLOWER SIZE: 1¹/₂ inches
BLOOM TIME: mid- to late summer
SOIL: moist, well drained
ZONES: 5-9

Arching wands are lined with clusters of fiery flowers for many weeks starting in midsummer. Though small, they're reminiscent of gladiolus flowers and they open from the base to the tip of the stem. The plant has a rather erect habit and thin, grassy leaves, so it's possible to fit crocosmia in and among bushier perennials and wait for its color show. A patch alongside a fence or wall is very impressive. Alternatively, feature it in a large pot on a patio or deck.

All crocosmia needs is moist, well-drained soil. It grows from small corms that should be set about 2 or 3 inches deep, and about 6 inches or more apart (crowding inhibits flowering). The vivid flowers are great for bouquets and last for a week or more; they can also be dried.

GOOD CHOICES: flame-red 'Lucifer' is outstanding; 'George Davidson' is a yellow version; large-flowered 'Columbus' has yellow-orange buds that open bright yellow

Daylily
Hemerocallis hybrids
MATURE HEIGHT × WIDTH: 1-3 feet × 1-3 feet
FLOWER COLORS: yellow, red, orange, pink, cream
FLOWER SIZE: 3-7 inches
BLOOM TIME: summer
SOIL: fertile, well drained
ZONES: 3-10

Ever-popular daylilies are an absolute "must" for anyone who wants plenty of easy-going color all summer long. All the plants ask is a sunny spot in fertile soil; many will do well in less sun and poorer ground. In return, you get fountains of trouble-free strappy green leaves and constant flowers.

Daylilies can be tucked into flower borders here and there for dependable, low-maintenance color. An entire bed, row, or ribbon of them looks beautiful, especially if you invest in a mix or choose a special cultivar to plant en masse. They can even be shown off in tubs or other containers, particularly the dwarf varieties. Every color with the exception of blue and pure white is available, with a variety of flower forms and sizes; browse the tantalizing array in the catalogs of specialty daylily nurseries. The industry award is called the Stout Medal; to start, you can look for winners.

GOOD CHOICES: the most widely grown daylily is the prolific, golden-flowered dwarf 'Stella d'Oro'; lemon-yellow 'Happy Returns' reblooms

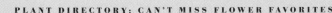

Delphinium
Delphinium elatum
MATURE HEIGHT × WIDTH: 4-8 feet × 2-3 feet
FLOWER COLORS: blue, purple, pink, white, bicolors
FLOWER SIZE: 2½-3 inches
BLOOM TIME: spring to summer
SOIL: fertile, moist, well drained
ZONES: 3-8

Their spires are magnificent, rising high in the early summer garden or as the centerpiece in a homegrown bouquet. If your summers are temperate (not too hot or humid), you should be able to grow gorgeous delphiniums.

First, pick a sunny spot out of the battering wind, perhaps against a fence or wall or at the back of a flower border. Next, prepare the soil just the way delphiniums like it: rich in organic matter. If the area is not naturally alkaline, add a handful of lime to each planting hole. Install a supporting stake that will reach at least up to the point the flowers begin (in most cases, about 5 feet tall). Don't mulch, as this invites rot.

GOOD CHOICES: heat- and humidity-tolerant New Millennium Hybrids include light blue 'Blue Lace', lime-tinged white 'Green Twist', and deep purple with a white center bee 'Purple Passion'; the classic Pacific Hybrids include many fine varieties, often with contrasting white bees; 'Galahad' is white

False Blue Indigo
Baptisia australis
MATURE HEIGHT × WIDTH: 3-4 feet × 2-3 feet
FLOWER COLORS: blue
FLOWER SIZE: 1-2 inches
BLOOM TIME: early summer
SOIL: average, well drained
ZONES: 3-9

If you like blue in your flower garden, false blue indigo is a lovely, low-maintenance choice. It tolerates average to poor soil and drought, is never bothered by pests or diseases, and blooms profusely early every summer. The sprays of pea-like flowers (it is in the pea family, related to sweet peas) are brilliant blue and look terrific for several weeks. They're a beautiful, airy addition to bouquets, especially with pink roses or yellow daisy flowers.

This tough plant is able to tolerate dry spells because it sends down a long taproot into the ground. So site it where you want it to stay—not too close to a fence or wall or shrubbery, as moving it later is not a good idea, and you will be reluctant to chop back any of the good-looking foliage.

GOOD CHOICES: B. australis has blue flowers; closely related B. alba has white flowers; 'Purple Smoke' is a pretty hybrid with purplish stems and flowers

Foxglove
Digitalis purpurea
MATURE HEIGHT × **WIDTH: 3-5 feet** × **2-3 feet**
FLOWER COLORS: pink, peach, lavender, white
FLOWER SIZE: 1-3 inches
BLOOM TIME: early to midsummer
SOIL: moist, well drained
ZONES: 4-8

Stately yet easy-going foxgloves are a cottage-garden or perennial border "must-have" because their bloom spires, laden with pretty spotted and speckled tubular bells, are so beautiful. And they fit in so well with many other flowers, in full sun or partial shade, from bellflowers to roses to bleeding hearts. Technically, most foxgloves are biennial, meaning they have a two-year life cycle. They spend their first year developing rosettes of foliage, and send up their stunning flower spikes the following year. But foxgloves also avidly self-sow, so once you have them, you are never without them. New plants will pop up in places that will suit them best.

GOOD CHOICES: peachy-pink 'Apricot' is a beauty on tall 40-inch stalks; 'Foxy' is a pastel mix of 2-foot-tall plants; 'Alba' is a glorious white; Giant Shirley Mix is ideal for massing at the back of a border

Gaura
Gaura lindheimeri
MATURE HEIGHT × **WIDTH: 3-4 feet** × **1-3 feet**
FLOWER COLORS: white, pink, red
FLOWER SIZE: 1 inch
BLOOM TIME: summer
SOIL: well drained
ZONES: 6-9

Slender wands arise with willowy foliage, topped with delicate flowers. Those lower on the stem open first, which is a good time to pick if you are going to, so the show can continue indoors in your vase. Usually white, or pale pink, there are now darker pink and scarlet varieties available. The green leaves are sometimes tinged red; there's even a gaura with gold-variegated foliage, which adds sparkle. There are dwarf forms perfect for growing in containers, and the giant 'Dauphin' can reach 7 feet tall.

Once established, gaura is a champ in hot, dry summers. It remains in bloom a long time. Be advised, however, that it owes its drought tolerance to the development of a long, stringy taproot, which you should never tamper with by trying to move or divide the plant.

GOOD CHOICES: 'Crimson Butterflies' has reddish leaves, red stems, and hot pink flowers; 'So White' has pure white flowers and is shorter than the species, at 18 inches; 'Corrie's Gold' has gold-splashed leaves

Goldenrod
Solidago species
MATURE HEIGHT × WIDTH: 2-6 feet × 2-4 feet
FLOWER COLORS: yellow
FLOWER SIZE: 6-12 inch clusters
BLOOM TIME: midsummer to fall
SOIL: average to lean, well drained
ZONES: 3-9

In the past, goldenrod was a spectacular late-summer wild-flower admired mainly in meadows and at the seashore. When horticulturists took a closer look, they found plenty to admire and work with: a clump-forming, noninvasive growth habit, no pest problems, good cold hardiness, and the ability to tolerate average to poor soil and still look wonderful. Nowadays goldenrod can hardly be called a weed. It's a major player in many late-season flower displays, where it brings radiant plumes of golden color over a long bloom period.

Try goldenrod in borders with fall-blooming asters, where it complements their golden flower centers. It's also an excellent companion for purple-plumed Russian sage, which blooms at the same time. Naturally, it's great in bouquets with these plants as well!

GOOD CHOICES: *S. rugosa* 'Fireworks' is a fountain-like plant, 3 to 4 feet tall, that cascades with yellow plumes; dwarf *S. sphacelata* 'Golden Fleece' stays under 2 feet and carries its cheery sprays in a tidy, pyramidal fashion

Hardy Geranium
Geranium species and hybrids
MATURE HEIGHT × WIDTH: 1-2 feet × 1-2 feet
FLOWER COLORS: purple, blue, pink, white
FLOWER SIZE: 1-3 inches
BLOOM TIME: spring and summer
SOIL: well drained
ZONES: 5-9

Some of the most versatile perennials belong to this broad and charming group. Most geraniums are groundcovers or low mounding plants, suitable for the front of a flower border, for weaving in and amongst taller flowers, or even for container displays. Lovely, saucer-shaped flowers adorn them in late spring and on into summer; these come in various shades of purple and blue, as well as soft pink, bright pink, magenta, and white.

To look their best, hardy geraniums like to have decent, well-drained soil. Some like it a little moister; some tolerate drought. Full sun will work for some types, but afternoon shade keeps foliage from burning for most.

GOOD CHOICES: 'Johnson's Blue' and 'Brookside' are prolific sky-blue bloomers; 'Jolly Bee' has blue flowers with a white eye and is touted as blooming from May until October; delightful 'Ann Folkard' has perky magenta flowers; 'Rozanne' and 'Splish Splash' have bicolor violet-and-white blooms with purple veining and are heat tolerant

Hardy Mum
Dendranthema and *Chrysanthemum* hybrids

MATURE HEIGHT × WIDTH: 2-3 feet × 2-3 feet
FLOWER COLORS: yellow, white, pink, peach, bicolors
FLOWER SIZE: 3-6 inches
BLOOM TIME: late summer to late fall
SOIL: well drained
ZONES: 4-9

Good old mums are certainly a fall classic, and deservedly so. No other plant delivers such great looking flowers so far into fall, weathering fall rains, cold nights, and windy days with great pluck. It's too bad people replant them every year, that is, treat them like annuals, when many are perfectly hardy and resilient perennials that can be brought through to bloom another year, especially if you pinch them several times before midsummer. There are also recent introductions (or reintroductions of mums popular long ago) that bloom profusely on trailing stems, which are truly perennial.

GOOD CHOICES: 'Clara Curtis' is an old-fashioned pink form; 'Ryan's Daisy' and 'Ryan's Yellow' have soft-colored, cascading sprays of daisy-like blossoms; 'Mary Stoker' is pale yellow; mums in the Minn Series flower before frost, even in the far north

Hellebore
Helleborus orientalis

MATURE HEIGHT × WIDTH: 1 1/2 feet × 2 feet
FLOWER COLORS: many
FLOWER SIZE: 3-4 inches
BLOOM TIME: early spring
SOIL: fertile, moist, well drained
ZONES: 4-8

If you still consider early spring to be the province of daffodils, tulips, and the like, prepare to be dazzled. Hellebores are no more difficult to grow, and they are beautiful. Their unique flowers are usually nodding and saucer shaped, and come in a lovely range of colors: white, pink, pale green, rose, or purple. The petals are often speckled. And, unlike most spring bloomers, they remain in flower a very long time—sometimes from the day the snow begins to melt until late spring!

The flowers are long lasting and the succulent stems and foliage are equally durable. The plants thrive in humus-rich soil that drains well, and they hold their form and color in partial to full shade.

GOOD CHOICES: long-blooming Royal Heritage™ Mix is superb; the Phedar Select Strain emphasizes dark colors and spotted flowers; 'Atrorubens' is plum purple; 'Betty Ranicar' is a fluffy double white

Hollyhock
Alcea rosea
MATURE HEIGHT × WIDTH: 5-8 feet × 2-3 feet
FLOWER COLORS: white, pink, peach, red
FLOWER SIZE: 2-4 inches
BLOOM TIME: summer to fall
SOIL: well drained
ZONES: 3-8

This tall bloomer is the classic "cottage garden" plant for most people and, luckily, it is easy to grow. It does fine in any well-drained soil, in full or partial sun. The clumps are substantial and the stems are stately and unbranched. The best places for hollyhocks are beside fences or against walls, which show them off to best advantage and may save you the trouble of staking if the structures can lend a little support. Hollyhocks are not long-lived; some are strictly biennial, so you must let them self-sow or replant them.

Old-fashioned varieties have single, bell-shaped flowers, but some of the newer ones are double, or sport ruffled or fringed petal edges for more impact.

GOOD CHOICES: Old Barnyard Mix features a rainbow of single blooms on 5- to 6-foot stems; Summer Memories Mix is especially rust resistant and cold hardy; novelty selection 'Nigra' has maroon, almost black, single blooms; 'Crème de Cassis' has vanilla-white blooms with raspberry veining; Powder Puffs Mix is a rainbow of fluffy doubles

Hollyhock Mallow
Malva alcea
MATURE HEIGHT × WIDTH: 3-4 feet × 1-2 feet
FLOWER COLORS: white, pink
FLOWER SIZE: 1 1/2-2 inches
BLOOM TIME: summer
SOIL: well drained
ZONES: 4-8

Bouncy, easy-going hollyhock mallow is a summertime delight. Saucer-shaped flowers cover the bushy plants for much of the summer. Usually pink, they bring scads of color and informal good cheer to sunny spots. In pastel-themed borders, their dependable presence and long bloom period are invaluable; they look good in the company of summer phlox and blazing star, in particular. This plant is also suitable for a good, medium-sized pot, arrayed on a patio or the front steps.

Hollyhock mallow is a tough customer, too. It grows well in most soils so long as the drainage is good and the sunshine is ample. It tolerates drought well. Though not long-lived, it will self-sow, and seedlings reach blooming size quickly.

GOOD CHOICES: 'Fastigiata' has a more upright habit than the species and rose-pink flowers

Iris

Iris species

MATURE HEIGHT × WIDTH: 3-4 feet × 3-4 feet
FLOWER COLORS: white, pink, purple, yellow, bicolors
FLOWER SIZE: 2-4 inches
BLOOM TIME: early summer
SOIL: moist, well drained
ZONES: 4-8

Among the many colorful irises suitable for gardens are Siberian iris (*I. sibirica*) and Japanese iris (*I. ensata*). These are now available in many beautiful colors and bicolors, although the range is not as broad as with bearded iris. Nonetheless, some gardeners prefer them. They are generally healthy and trouble-free, asking little more than full sun and slightly moist, organically rich soil to show off. The Siberian flowers are smaller and narrower, while those of the Japanese varieties are fairly broad and splay outward.

Both types are particularly impressive when massed. And the foliage is more narrow and grass-like than that of bearded iris, so they slip unobtrusively into the flower-border background when no longer in bloom.

GOOD CHOICES: for Siberian iris, seek out the perky white-and-yellow 'Butter & Sugar' or the vivid violet 'Caesar's Brother'; among Japanese irises, deep purple 'Black Knight' is gorgeous, as is violet-white-mulberry 'Flying Tiger'

Japanese Anemone

Anemone × *hybrida*

MATURE HEIGHT × WIDTH: 3-5 feet × 2-3 feet
FLOWER COLORS: pink, white
FLOWER SIZE: 2-4 inches
BLOOM TIME: late summer to fall
SOIL: fertile, moist, well drained
ZONES: 5-7

Late-season pink or white isn't easy to come by, but if you are seeking an alternative to fall's reds, yellows, and oranges, this dependable bloomer can set a different tone in your flower garden. For most of the summer, the plant is a medium to large mound of good-looking green foliage, but by August, slender stalks arise, topped with appealing, simple, daisy-like flowers. The plant is sometimes called "windflower," which refers to the way these pretty blooms toss in the breeze.

The flowers show up better if there is a backdrop, such as a dark wall, fence, or hedge, so keep that in mind when looking around your yard for a good place to plant them. They also like to have organically rich soil.

GOOD CHOICES: 'Queen Charlotte' has silvery pink, double blooms; those of 'Honorine Jobert' are white; novelty 'Whirlwind' has semi-double, fluffy white flowers

PERENNIALS AND BIENNIALS

Joe-Pye Weed
Eupatorium maculatum

MATURE HEIGHT × WIDTH: 4-6 feet × 2-4 feet
FLOWER COLORS: mauve
FLOWER SIZE: 6-10 inch clusters
BLOOM TIME: summer to early fall
SOIL: moist, well drained
ZONES: 3-10

It seems unfair to call this exciting, tall bloomer a weed, for it makes a magnificent contribution to the late-summer garden, at a time when you wish you had more color in the landscape. Because it hails from wet, sunny meadows, it does prefer full sun and damp ground in cultivation. Other than that, it is easy to grow and always delights. The big, frothy flower heads are a magnet for butterflies, too.

Because it takes up a lot of space, your best bet is to site Joe-Pye weed along a fence, along a garage wall, or at the back of a mixed flower border. When it's not in bloom, the handsome, toothed leaves and wine-red stems remain an asset.

GOOD CHOICES: 'Gateway' is shorter, has darker purple flowers, and darker stems

Lavender
Lavandula angustifolia

MATURE HEIGHT × WIDTH: 2-3 feet × 2-3 feet
FLOWER COLORS: purple
FLOWER SIZE: 4-6 inch spikes
BLOOM TIME: late spring to summer
SOIL: well drained
ZONES: 5-9

Carefree, eager-blooming, fragrant lavender has left the herb garden far behind. You now see it as an edging plant, in mixed borders, among roses, in rock gardens, as a short hedge, and even in decorative pots and planter boxes. The newer varieties have an attractive, tidy growth habit and the flower spires are better than ever in terms of flower size and density as well as that coveted fragrance. In short, lavender has become an outstanding plant for today's flower gardens.

Full sun is best. As for the soil, any well-drained ground will do (soggy soil leads to rot). If the pH is a little alkaline, so much the better; if not, you can nudge it that way by adding lime dust or lime chips to the planting area. As for maintenance, shearing or clipping lavender is a pleasant chore and one from which the plant recovers quickly.

GOOD CHOICES: 'Hidcote Superior' is especially compact and heavy blooming; old favorite 'Munstead' has a neat form and lavender-blue spires; 'Silver Edge' is similar but has white-rimmed foliage for extra appeal

Lily-of-the-Valley
Convallaria majalis
MATURE HEIGHT × WIDTH: 6-12 inches × 1-2 feet
FLOWER COLORS: white, pink
FLOWER SIZE: 3/8 inch
BLOOM TIME: mid-spring
SOIL: moist, well drained
ZONES: 2-7

Lupine
Lupinus hybrids
MATURE HEIGHT × WIDTH: 3-4 feet × 1 1/2-2 feet
FLOWER COLORS: blue, red, pink, white, yellow, bicolors
FLOWER SIZE: 1-2 inches
BLOOM TIME: late spring to early summer
SOIL: moist, well drained
ZONES: 4-8

For a weed-excluding groundcover for shady or semi-shady areas or under trees, lily-of-the-valley is hard to beat. The wide, lance-shaped leaves grow more and more thickly as the years go by. There are no serious pests or diseases to worry about.

But all practical concerns aside, it is the darling little flowers that make us love this plant. Present for many weeks every spring, they emerge from the leaves on slender, arching stems and look like tiny, chubby bells. They waft a delicious scent over your garden. Some people like to pick them for sweet little bouquets; there are certainly always plenty to spare. If you can find it, the pink-flowered version is a pretty alternative.

GOOD CHOICES: the white-flowered species has been popular for centuries; the pink version is called 'Rosea'

Stately and beautiful, lupines are a splendid border perennial in the Pacific Northwest, the Northeast, and in cool mountain areas in other parts of the country. They need cool, damp weather and fertile, moist, organically rich soil that is slightly acidic to reach their full, spectacular potential. In such areas and conditions, however, they are easy to grow well.

Plant breeders have been issuing a steady stream of excellent new hybrids and mixes. The tall, dense spires now come in creamy white, lemon yellow, peppermint pink, scarlet, royal blue, and deep purple, as well as bicolors with contrasting white. Even the leaves are pretty—palmate leaves made of lance-shaped leaflets. Rainwater beads up on their silky-hairy surfaces.

GOOD CHOICES: Russell Hybrids are the classic mix; New Generations Hybrids are also excellent; the Gallery Series features shorter ones, reaching only 15 to 18 inches; 'Chantelaine' has pink and white flowers

Marguerite
Anthemis tinctoria
MATURE HEIGHT × WIDTH: 1½-3 feet × 2½ feet
FLOWER COLORS: yellow, white
FLOWER SIZE: 2 inches
BLOOM TIME: summer
SOIL: average, well drained
ZONES: 3-7

A handsome, low-maintenance plant, marguerite is a true yellow-flowered daisy for late season color. It produces numerous small flowers for up to two months, even longer if you deadhead regularly, or better yet, pick bouquets. Give it a spot in full sun and lean soil.

The plant is rather casual, bushy, and sprawling, so it belongs where you want a more exuberant, wild look. No pests or diseases ever trouble it, and mildew only appears when air circulation is poor, a problem easily remedied by not crowding it. Butterflies may visit also.

GOOD CHOICES: 'E.C. Buxton' has almost-white flowers; those of 'Moonlight' are soft, pale yellow

Monkshood
Aconitum napellus
MATURE HEIGHT × WIDTH: 3-4 feet × 2 feet
FLOWER COLORS: blue, purple, white, pink
FLOWER SIZE: 1-2 inches
BLOOM TIME: mid- to late summer
SOIL: fertile, moist, well drained
ZONES: 4-8

Spires of deep blue rise above handsome, rich green leaves on tall, slender stems. Staking might be required. They make an impressive showing toward the back of a flower border and bloom in the latter part of the summer, sometimes continuing on into fall. They fare better in areas with cooler summers.

The back of the border, or at least behind other plants, is a wise placement for another reason—unfortunately, every part of this plant is poisonous, and you certainly don't want children or pets to take an interest in it. That said, monkshood is still a gorgeous sight, especially since it is a late-season bloomer. Late-flowering yellow perennials, of which there are quite a few (sunflowers, black-eyed Susans, sneezeweeds) make fine companions. Just be sure monkshood gets the moisture it needs.

GOOD CHOICES: the species is a rich blue; 'Album' is the white version; 'Rubellum' sports soft pink flowers and reaches 40 inches high

Penstemon
Penstemon species
MATURE HEIGHT × WIDTH: 2-4 feet × 1-3 feet
FLOWER COLORS: purple, red, pink, white
FLOWER SIZE: 1-2 inches
BLOOM TIME: midsummer to fall
SOIL: well drained
ZONES: 4-8

Penstemon's vivacious colors always bring welcome excitement to midsummer. Its stems are adorned with loose racemes of beautiful, tubular flowers for much of the summer. The cultivated varieties are fabulous, exhibiting larger flowers, richer flower color, and more numerous flowers, for greater garden impact. And hummingbirds cannot resist penstemon flowers! As for the plants, they have long, thin, lance- or spoon-shaped leaves and a loose, shrubby habit, so they fit easily into a perennial border.

Like their wild forebears, most of which are native to the western U.S., garden penstemons are durable and tough. They like full sun, tolerate lean soil so long as it is well drained, survive drought, and bloom prolifically.

GOOD CHOICES: *P. digitalis* 'Husker Red', the PPA winner in 1996, sports pink-tinged white flowers and reddish foliage and stems; the flowers of 'Donna' are vibrant, long-lasting pink; 'Mother of Pearl' has the perfect name to describe its lovely white-tinged-purple flowers

Peony
Paeonia lactiflora
MATURE HEIGHT × WIDTH: 1-3 feet × 2-3 feet
FLOWER COLORS: white, pink, red
FLOWER SIZE: 3-5 inches
BLOOM TIME: spring
SOIL: fertile, moist, well drained
ZONES: 3-7

Plush, hauntingly fragrant flowers—what would springtime be without luscious peonies? They can be grown even in the coldest climates and come through tough winters handily. And although there are tried-and-true old-fashioned favorites, recent years have seen a flurry of new introductions that are worth looking into. Some of these have novel flower forms. Plant breeders have also made significant improvements to stem strength, so that the big flowers won't hang their heads in the rain.

To get the best display, plant them the previous fall in organically rich soil. Take care that you don't sink the "eyes" on the root clumps any more than a 2 inches below the soil surface. If your winters are cold, mulch to prevent frost heaving. In early spring, stake or provide "peony hoops."

GOOD CHOICES: double white, crimson-flecked 'Festiva Maxima' is a classic; 'Karl Rosenfeld' is ruby red; 'Sorbet' is soft, romantic pink; 'Raspberry Sundae' has a fluffy vanilla interior

Perennial Sunflower
Helianthus × multiflorus (H. decapetalus)
MATURE HEIGHT × WIDTH: 4-6 feet × 2-3 feet
FLOWER COLORS: yellow
FLOWER SIZE: 3-5 inches
BLOOM TIME: midsummer to fall
SOIL: well drained
ZONES: 5-9

Perhaps not what you usually imagine when you think of sunflowers—the tall, open-faced annuals (see *Helianthus annuus*)—but these can have the same impact in the late summer garden. The species produce lots and lots of bright yellow daisies, up to 5 inches across. The cultivars and hybrids are also interesting, with the same-size flowers, but in double, pom-pom form, dense and fluffy with many petals. Single or double, these terrific sunflowers burst on the scene in the latter part of the summer and add brightness and exuberance to your garden. The plants are clump-formers, bushy with coarse, long, dark green leaves. They can still get tall, and wide, so you need to allot them ample room.

GOOD CHOICES: the sunny yellow flowers of double 'Flore Pleno' really stand out; those of 'Loddon Gold' are up to 6 inches across and more gold than yellow

Peruvian Lily
Alstroemeria species and hybrids
MATURE HEIGHT × WIDTH: 1½-2 feet × 2½ feet
FLOWER COLORS: yellow, red, white, purple
FLOWER SIZE: 1½-4 inches
BLOOM TIME: summer
SOIL: fertile, moist, well drained
ZONES: 6-10

It used to be that you only saw these elegant, long-stemmed members of the lily family at the florist, where you learned that they are especially long-lasting cut flowers. But, as gardeners in mild climates now know and those in other areas are discovering, Peruvian lilies are not difficult to grow at home. If you don't want to try them in the ground or your growing season is short, you can raise them in pots.

Here's what they need: organically rich soil that drains well, regular watering, and warm sunshine. They grow from brittle tubers, which should be planted deeply, about 8 inches. You should mulch to retain soil moisture. They don't like being exposed to the wind, or extremes of heat and cold, so site them in a sheltered spot.

GOOD CHOICES: hybrids of *A. ligtu* are gorgeous pastels; newer hybrid 'Sweet Laura' is hardy to Zone 6 and sports golden blooms with mahogany markings plus a delicate scent; peachy-red 'Freedom' is a beauty and also tolerates summer humidity well

Pincushion Flower
Scabiosa columbaria
MATURE HEIGHT × WIDTH: 1-2 feet × 1-2 feet
FLOWER COLORS: lavender, blue, pink
FLOWER SIZE: 2-3 inches
BLOOM TIME: summer
SOIL: slightly alkaline, well drained
ZONES: 5-9

Disk-shaped clusters of lacy blooms cover this splendid plant for most of the summer. The plant, never too big or leggy, is in keeping with the flowers' airiness, sporting slightly fuzzy stems and small leaflets of sage green. This perennial is an excellent choice for tucking into flowerbeds here and there just to be sure there is always color in your garden. The colors go well with almost every other flower; the pink form is a soft, endearing hue, and the lavender-blue version is quite versatile.

Pincushion flower is happy and healthy when given lots of sun and provided with well-drained soil that is slightly alkaline. Cut the blooms for old-fashioned charm in mixed bouquets, or snip them off after they fade on the plant, and you can be sure there will be plenty more to follow. But be careful—the spent flower heads and unopened new flower clusters look very similar.

GOOD CHOICES: 'Butterfly Blue' was the PPA winner in 2000; 'Pink Mist' is the pink version

Pinks
Dianthus species
MATURE HEIGHT × WIDTH: 6-12 inches × 1 foot
FLOWER COLORS: white, pink, red
FLOWER SIZE: 1-2 inches
BLOOM TIME: late spring to midsummer
SOIL: moist, well drained
ZONES: 3-8

These jaunty, spicily scented flowers come in pink, red, and white. The common name refers to the fringed or ragged edges of the petals, as if they had been trimmed with miniature pinking shears. Though their peak bloom is early in the season, they'll keep flowering if you pick them for small bouquets or remember to deadhead regularly.

Excellent drainage is a must, since soggy ground inhibits their growth and flowering. It's not a good idea to mulch their crowns. Instead, you can surround their bases with gravel. Slightly alkaline soil is preferred, but if your garden lacks that condition, you can sprinkle a few lime chips in the vicinity in spring. Problems with pests and diseases are blessedly rare. Full sun brings out the best in pinks.

GOOD CHOICES: *D. gratianopolitanus* 'Bath's Pink' is adapted to high heat and humidity; *D. deltoides* 'Zing Rose' is a vibrant rosy red; 'Betty Morton' has larger, hot pink blooms; 'Snowbank' is a fluffy white flower with intense fragrance

Poppy
Papaver orientale
MATURE HEIGHT × WIDTH: 2-4 feet × 2-3 feet
FLOWER COLORS: red, pink, white, orange
FLOWER SIZE: 3-4 inches
BLOOM TIME: early summer
SOIL: fertile, moist, well drained
ZONES: 3-8

Though their bloom time is all too short—a mere week or two early every summer—poppies are so extraordinarily showy and beautiful that gardeners adore them. Big, goblet-shaped, and graced with an irresistible crepe-paper texture (that is more durable than you might think), they come in dreamy colors. Some are purest orange, some are brilliant red, and some are watermelon pink. The petal bases have contrasting black spots and the central ring of fuzzy dark stamens adds drama.

One poppy plant perched at the base of a fence or stone wall can stop traffic. Integrated into a border, poppies look grand with blue flowers such as bellflowers, false blue indigo, or bluestar, as well as lupines. Eventually the petals shatter and the rough foliage lingers for a while until the plant goes dormant. The show is over, but it was all worth it.

GOOD CHOICES: 'Patty's Plum' is an exceptional plum-purple; aptly named 'Glowing Embers' is red-orange; 'Juliana' is a lovely pink

Red-Hot Poker
Kniphofia species
MATURE HEIGHT × WIDTH: 2-4 feet × 1-2 feet
Flower Colors: red, yellow, orange, cream
Flower Size: 6-10 inch spikes
Bloom Time: summer
Soil: well drained
Zones: 6-9

Every summer, above dense clumps of long, grass-like leaves, arise the most striking flower spikes. The colors are usually bright and fiery, in the red-orange-yellow range, changing color as the flowers fade. A bicolor effect occurs when the tubular blossoms on each taper open and age from the bottom up. At that point, neighbors will be peeking over your garden fence and hummingbirds will be coming by for a visit.

For successful growth, site your red-hot pokers in the bright sunshine in well-drained soil; soggy ground is bad news. The plants look great in small groups or massed at an entryway or along a low fence. If the colors are too bright for your garden plans, consider some of the pastel cultivars or a pale yellow variety.

GOOD CHOICES: hot-color mix 'Flamenco'; vanilla-white, shorter (to 20 inches) 'Little Maid'; dark orange to light orange 'Drummore Apricot' is sensational; the flowers of 'Nancy's Red' are luscious coral-red

Rose Mallow
Hibiscus moscheutos
MATURE HEIGHT × WIDTH: 3-5 feet × 5 feet
FLOWER COLORS: white, pink, red, bicolors
FLOWER SIZE: 6-12 inches
BLOOM TIME: summer
SOIL: moist, well drained
ZONES: 4-9

A tall, bushy, fast-growing plant, rose mallow has dramatic flowers with bottlebrush centers. In fact, it may have the largest flowers in this genus—some of the hybrids carry dinner plate-size ones that reach upwards of 12 inches across. Individual plants make dramatic garden focal points.

Because this plant is found in wet areas and along streams in nature, you need to give it good soil moisture or regular watering, plus a protective mulch around the roots, or deliberately site it in a low, wet spot. A little shelter from drying winds is a good idea, too. Regular fertilizing will assure tremendous flowering.

GOOD CHOICES: 'Southern Belle' is a nice mix of red, pink, and white; 'Lord Baltimore' has huge 10-inch brilliant red flowers; the Disco Series has large flowers on compact plants; light pink 'Kopper King' has contrasting burgundy leaves that are an asset to the garden even when the plant isn't blooming

Russian Sage
Perovskia atriplicifolia
MATURE HEIGHT × WIDTH: 3-4 feet × 2-3 feet
FLOWER COLORS: lavender-blue
FLOWER SIZE: 12-inch panicles
BLOOM TIME: summer
SOIL: well drained
ZONES: 4-9

A well-grown Russian sage plant is a breathtaking sight. It has a shrub-like form, with long stems of aromatic leaves spraying upward and outward in all directions from the central crown, each stem laden with lovely small flowers. The leaves are gray-green, like sage, and the flowers are lilac-purple—the contrast is just beautiful.

If you have a big-enough place in full sun, Russian sage is very easy to grow. Pests, including nibbling deer, and diseases are unknown. It blooms most of the summer, and if you pick stems for bouquets, they are soon replaced. You should cut it down early every spring if last year's stems remain, so it can renew itself for another great year.

GOOD CHOICES: the species won the PPA award in 1995; 'Little Spires', at about 2 feet, is suitable for smaller spaces; 'Longin' is a bit more compact than the species and has violet spires

PERENNIALS AND BIENNIALS

Salvia
Salvia species and hybrids
MATURE HEIGHT × WIDTH: 1-5 feet × 2-4 feet
FLOWER COLORS: blue, purple, red, pink, white
FLOWER SIZE: 12-15 inch racemes
BLOOM TIME: summer
SOIL: well drained
ZONES: 4-8

This is a big group of flowering perennials, and they're not the culinary herb at all, though their leaves may be just as aromatic and they are still perfectly edible. Ornamental salvias have become extremely popular in sunny gardens in recent years because the selections are superb. Some are as tall as 4 to 5 feet, others are good mid-border choices at 12 to 18 inches high. Some prefer moist soil to look their best, while others are remarkably drought-tolerant. All are long blooming.

Salvias are a particularly good source of the sought-after blue to purple hues. They are also good cut flowers, particularly in mixed bouquets.

GOOD CHOICES: indigo-blue flowers adorn 'May Night', the PPA winner in 1997; 'Rose Queen' is similar, but with rose-pink flowers; *S. guaranitica* 'Indigo Spires' is tall with dark blue flowers

Sedum
Sedum species
MATURE HEIGHT × WIDTH: 1-2 feet × 1-2 feet
FLOWER COLORS: white, pink, lavender, red
FLOWER SIZE: 3-6 inch clusters
BLOOM TIME: late summer
SOIL: well drained
ZONES: 4-9

Autumn's rich, earthy tones signal cooling temperatures and the winding down of the gardening year. Many of us grow the classic, rosy-red 'Autumn Joy' especially for this moment. But you will be intrigued to learn that there are many superb sedums that have the same handsome appearance (including the changing flower colors from summer into fall) but in improved and perhaps more beautiful shades. Horticulturists have also been selecting for interesting, colored foliage on these plants. For instance, newer 'Matrona' has pink-rimmed gray leaves and soft pink flowers. The hot pink flowers of 'Neon' are as bright as the name implies.

GOOD CHOICES: 'Autumn Joy' remains a standard; pink-flowered 'Matrona'; hot pink 'Neon'; 'Vera Jameson' has rich rosy pink blooms against smoky blue foliage

Shasta Daisy

Leucanthemum* × *superbum

MATURE HEIGHT × WIDTH: 1-3½ feet × 2-3 feet
FLOWER COLORS: white
FLOWER SIZE: 2-3 inches
BLOOM TIME: summer to fall
SOIL: fertile, moist, well drained
ZONES: 5-9

Here's the best and brightest classic daisy there is. You might grow it just for the armloads of bouquets you wish to harvest, for the plants are definitely prolific. Or you might incorporate a plant here and there in your perennial beds, where its spunky color and good health are valuable. Alternatively, you could mass it in the front of your house in a sunny bed.

It does need proper growing conditions, however, in order to deliver that fantastic performance. The soil should be organically rich and drain well (soggy ground causes this daisy to falter and perhaps even succumb over the winter months). The spot should also be sunny, unless your summers are blazingly hot, in which case a little afternoon shade is welcome. Finally, you should water regularly and deadhead or cut bouquets often.

GOOD CHOICES: heat-tolerant 'Becky' was the PPA winner in 2003; the big flowers of 'Alaska' are flawless; 'Silver Princess' is a shorter plant, from 12 to 15 inches

Spike Speedwell

Veronica spicata

MATURE HEIGHT × WIDTH: 1-2 feet × 1-2 feet
FLOWER COLORS: blue, white, pink
FLOWER SIZE: 8-12 inch spikes
BLOOM TIME: summer
SOIL: average, well drained
ZONES: 4-9

This is a super plant for dependable color! Spike speedwell does your garden proud with dense, beautiful flower spikes starting in early summer and continuing for at least two months, longer if you take the time to deadhead. The plant has a neat, upright habit that allows you to tuck it into any number of places in a border, or to use a row of them as an edging. You can even grow a plant or two in a pot, and count on it to always look good. And the stems are long enough so you can snip a few to include in bouquets.

Usually a fine shade of blue, spike speedwell also comes in other colors, including rosy red and white, further extending its potential in your borders. All it requires is moderately fertile, well-drained soil. Though excellent in full sun, it tolerates some shade.

GOOD CHOICES: 'Sunny Border Blue', the PPA winner in 1993, is justly popular for its excellent form and deep color; 'Red Fox' is rosy red; perky 'White Icicle' is on the tall side; pretty 'Minuet' has pink spikes on gray-green foliage

PERENNIALS AND BIENNIALS

Summer Phlox
Phlox paniculata
MATURE HEIGHT × WIDTH: 2-5 feet × 2 feet
FLOWER COLORS: purple, pink, red, white, bicolors
FLOWER SIZE: 10-12 inch clusters
BLOOM TIME: summer
SOIL: fertile, moist, well drained
ZONES: 3-9

Lush, dome-shaped flower clusters, like big ice-cream cones, top tall summer phlox plants for most of the summer. The wide-ranging colors and bicolors are wonderful, bright and cheerful in the hot summer sun. Plus, the flowers are deliciously fragrant. Using a single color or variety in a grouping is sensational. Or add a few plants here and there throughout a flowerbed for their bright, reliable color.

Traditionally, the foliage has been disfigured by powdery mildew. Spacing the clumps a couple of feet apart improves air circulation. You should also always make a practice of watering the plants at ground level (to avoid getting the foliage wet), and get rid of dead foliage every fall. But the good news is that many impressive, highly mildew-resistant cultivars are now available.

GOOD CHOICES: mildew-resistant, pure white 'David' was the PPA winner in 2002; 'Tracy's Treasure' has soft pink flowers; 'Laura' has white-eyed fuchsia-pink blooms

Valerian
Centranthus ruber
MATURE HEIGHT × WIDTH: 1-3 feet × 1-2 feet
FLOWER COLORS: red, pink, white
FLOWER SIZE: 3-inch clusters
BLOOM TIME: summer
SOIL: average, well drained, alkaline
ZONES: 5-8

Here's a plant that's very tough and resilient, and self-sows around your yard over the years. Valerian offers terrific, easy color over most of the summer—and the flowers are so handsome, that you will find yourself clipping some to add to your bouquets. It usually comes in bright pink, but there are a few good cultivars, notably a clean, bright white and a raspberry red.

In the wild valerian, or Jupiter's beard, is found in rocky places and limestone soils; if you have these conditions in your yard, it will find a happy home. But such conditions are not required—it will do fine in most average, well-drained sites, and tolerates summer drought.

GOOD CHOICES: 'Albus' is a fine white; 'Coccineus' is raspberry-red

Virginia Bluebells
Mertensia virginica
MATURE HEIGHT × WIDTH: 1-2 feet × 1½ feet
FLOWER COLORS: blue, pink, white
FLOWER SIZE: 1 inch
BLOOM TIME: mid- to late spring
SOIL: fertile, well drained
ZONES: 3-7

Native to shade-dappled woodlands, this wildflower makes a wonderful garden plant. Groups of pink buds open into blue tubular flowers; on every plant, some are in bud, others are not quite open, and some are fully open, creating a very charming bicolor effect. The plant is sufficiently tall to stand out in the shade garden. Virginia bluebells is an ideal companion for bulbs, not just because of its compatible colors but because it likes the same conditions; the generous clumps of leaves can help disguise the foliage of early blooming bulbs as it begins to yellow and die back.

By early summer, as trees or shrubs overhead create a thicker canopy, Virginia bluebells begins to flag and become dormant, disappearing from view. But it will be back in glory next spring, so if you continue to plant in that part of the garden, be sure to mark its spot so you don't damage its fleshy underground rootstock.

GOOD CHOICES: the species is more commonly available, but 'Alba' has white flowers that sparkle in dim areas

Yarrow
Achillea millefolium
MATURE HEIGHT × WIDTH: 2-3 feet × 2-3 feet
FLOWER COLORS: yellow, white, red, pink
FLOWER SIZE: 4-5 inch clusters
BLOOM TIME: summer
SOIL: well drained
ZONES: 4-8

Yarrow has received well-deserved attention in recent years and there are many excellent cultivars on the market. As a plant, it has much to offer: a long bloom period (even in hot, dry summers); pest or disease problems are rare; and a medium-size, informal form that fits well in mixed borders. The handsome, finely dissected leaves are gray-green and lightly aromatic.

As a flower, yarrow is equally appealing, with flat-topped clusters of blooms that are dependably attractive. The common yellow and white versions are easily found, but you might also enjoy growing a rose or red one, or a pastel mix (available from many seed companies). Yarrow also makes an appealing, long-lasting cut flower, fresh as well as dried.

GOOD CHOICES: peppery-red 'Paprika'; 1990 AAS winner 'Summer Pastels' is a lovely mix; hybrid 'Fanal' has red flowers with yellow centers; pink 'Heidi' can rebloom later in the summer

Flowering
Shrubs

No garden should be without shrubs. A large property needs them for the mass and year-round interest they provide so well. A small yard gains dimension and character with the inclusion of at least a few shrubs. It's enjoyable to watch them change with the seasons, and because they are long-lived, you know they are with you for the long haul. Their scale allows them to be enjoyed at eye level, and they combine well with perennials, annuals, bulbs, and trees.

Flowering shrubs are the best type to have, no matter how big or small your garden. Some are long bloomers and some are brief, but their period of glory is always memorable and something to eagerly anticipate each year. Shrubs can have splendid flowers, in a unique form or special color. Some attract butterflies or waft a sweet or spicy fragrance. Some flowering shrubs bestow pretty extras, from handsome dried flowers to berries to fiery fall foliage. The ones described in the following pages have captured the admiration and imagination of many gardeners, and some of them may find a home in your yard.

Andromeda
Pieris species
MATURE HEIGHT × WIDTH: 6 feet × 6 feet
FLOWER COLORS: white, pink, red
FLOWER SIZE: 5-inch clusters
BLOOM TIME: spring
SOIL: fertile, moist, well drained
ZONES: 5-8

A handsome broadleaf shrub, andromeda requires acidic, moist, well-drained soil, like its cousins the rhododendrons and mountain laurels. With those needs met, it becomes a gracefully arching shrub that enhances borders and foundation plantings. The faintly fragrant, small white flowers are displayed in pendulous panicles that are charming—when pieris plants are massed, the effect is dramatic. Do not make the mistake of pruning this beautiful shrub. It looks much better when allowed to grow into its natural form and display its profusion of flowers every spring.

GOOD CHOICES: 'Mountain Fire' has fiery red new growth and lush white flowers (quite a show!); 'Flamingo' is a good (non-fading) red-flowered one; 'Valley Rose' has pastel pink blooms against glossy green leaves

Azalea
Rhododendron species and hybrids
MATURE HEIGHT × WIDTH: 4-12 feet × 2-6 feet
FLOWER COLORS: white, yellow, pink, orange, red
FLOWER SIZE: 2-3 inches
BLOOM TIME: spring
SOIL: average, well drained
ZONES: 5-8

Azaleas come in two forms, evergreen and deciduous. The deciduous ones are most common and generally hardier than their evergreen cousins, and their pretty spring flowers sometimes come with a pleasing scent. But the evergreen ones are also appealing. They bear masses of the bright blooms for which the group is famous, on handsome, compact shrubs that hold their leaves all winter. The catch is hardiness: Many won't survive chilly winters.

Because most azaleas don't have a prolonged bloom period, it's good to make the most of it. Plant early perennials or spring-blooming bulbs (daffodils, for instance) that look nice with the azalea colors you've chosen.

GOOD CHOICES: among deciduous azaleas, 'Northern Lights' is excellent, sporting flowers of various shades of pink; for vivid orange, seek out 'Gilbraltar'; among evergreen ones, anything with "Girard" in the name ('Girard Fuchsia', 'Girard Pleasant White', and so on) is good; double-flowered, silvery pink 'Rosebud' is lovely

FLOWERING SHRUBS

Beautybush
Kolkwitzia amabilis
MATURE HEIGHT × WIDTH: 8-10 feet × 6-8 feet
FLOWER COLORS: pink, red
FLOWER SIZE: ¹/₂ inch
BLOOM TIME: late spring to early summer
SOIL: average, well drained
ZONES: 5-8

This old-fashioned shrub fell out of favor for a time but is increasing in popularity once again. Sweet clusters of small, yellow-centered, pink, bell-shaped flowers appear in abundance late every spring and linger into the first weeks of summer—a very pretty sight. Bristly pinkish-brown seedpods follow, creating interest for a few more weeks. New flower buds form after that, so prune the bush right as the flowers are fading or only sparingly, or you'll reduce next year's show. This is an arching, rambling bush that brings carefree charm to a low-maintenance garden. Since it can become quite large, it also makes a good screening plant. It grows best in full sun, where it maintains a more dense form; in too much shade it can look twiggy. It adapts to most any soil.

GOOD CHOICES: 'Pink Cloud' has especially deep pink flowers; 'Rosea' flowers are rosy red

Blue Mist Shrub
Caryopteris × clandonensis
MATURE HEIGHT × WIDTH: 2 feet × 2 feet
FLOWER COLORS: blue, purple
FLOWER SIZE: ¹/₂ inch
BLOOM TIME: late summer to early fall
SOIL: well drained
ZONES: 6-9

How wonderful it is to get bountiful blue color late in the summer and on into the fall! Blue mist looks great with late-season reds, oranges, and yellows, whether from autumn leaves or nearby late-blooming perennials. Meanwhile, butterflies drop by for a visit and the gray-green foliage wafts a faint fragrance.

As a garden plant, blue mist is very easygoing. It likes full sun and tolerates average to dry soil. You may treat it more like a perennial, however, cutting it back in early spring and letting a flush of new growth and flowers form.

GOOD CHOICES: widely grown 'Dark Knight' has excellent, deep blue flowers; those of 'Blue Mist' are powder blue; 'Worcester Gold' has chartreuse foliage

Bottlebrush
Callistemon citrinus
MATURE HEIGHT × WIDTH: 10-15 feet × 5-7 feet
FLOWER COLORS: red
FLOWER SIZE: 4-inch clusters
BLOOM TIME: summer
SOIL: average, well drained
ZONES: 9-11

For mild climates, it's difficult to find a better long-blooming shrub. (In colder climates, it may be grown well in a large container.) Numerous large, fuzzy "bottlebrush" blooms adorn the plant from spring to fall. Hummingbirds cannot resist! The leaves start off in spring a reddish color, but soon turn green. When crushed, they have a distinctly lemony scent, hence the "citrinus" part of the botanical name. Though naturally dense—making it ideal for boundary plantings and shrub borders bottlebrush tolerates shaping and pruning very well. Just give it a spot in full sun, and enjoy!

GOOD CHOICES: 'Splendens' has outrageously large carmine-red blooms; 'Compacta', as the name suggests, is a smaller version, staying within 4 feet by 4 feet

Bottlebrush Buckeye
Aesculus parviflora
MATURE HEIGHT × WIDTH: 8-12 feet × 9-12 feet
FLOWER COLORS: white
FLOWER SIZE: 8-12 inch clusters
BLOOM TIME: midsummer
SOIL: moist, well drained
ZONES: 5-8

Here's something of a rarity: a shrub whose peak bloom is in summer, but which also performs beautifully in shade. If you have a dim area under trees in your yard that you have been struggling to brighten up, this may be your plant. The flowers are spectacular—they're borne in bottlebrush clusters and are white, with red anthers protruding to make a handsome show. The dark, somewhat coarse foliage shows them off to good advantage. (Later, in fall, the leaves turn golden yellow.)

The plant's only drawback, depending on where you site it, is its habit of spreading via suckers. If you don't want a thicket, you can clip off the unwanted stems as they appear. In more sun the leaves also have a tendency to droop during the heat of midday, but this is normal and they will revive by afternoon.

GOOD CHOICES: the species is the most commonly available; 'Rogers' has longer flower clusters and blooms later

FLOWERING SHRUBS

Broom
Cytisus × praecox
MATURE HEIGHT × WIDTH: 4-6 feet × 4-6 feet
FLOWER COLORS: cream, yellow, pink
FLOWER SIZE: ¹/₂ inch
BLOOM TIME: spring
SOIL: average to dry, well drained
ZONES: 6-9

A broom bush in full and glorious bloom is a sight to see. The arching branches fountain outwards, enveloped in small pea-like flowers; flower arrangers like to clip the stems for handsome filler in bouquets. Some gardeners grow broom in quantity, as a boundary or foundation hedge, but a single, well-placed plant can be quite spectacular in its own right, especially when backlit by late-afternoon sun.

No matter what you decide, be sure to place broom in a warm, sunny spot. It doesn't need fussing: no real pruning, minimal fertilizing, and occasional water in very dry spells is all. The flowers may have a slight, pungent scent.

GOOD CHOICES: 'Albus' has white flowers; those of 'Allgold' are deep yellow; those of 'Gold Spear' are bright, sunny yellow; 'Hollandia' has bicolor hot pink/pale pink blossoms

Butterfly Bush
Buddleia davidii
MATURE HEIGHT × WIDTH: 6-12 feet × 6-12 feet
FLOWER COLORS: blue, purple, red, pink, white
FLOWER SIZE: 4-10 inch clusters
BLOOM TIME: early summer
SOIL: fertile, well drained
ZONES: 5-9

Butterfly bush is often used as a hedge but it can also be used as an outstanding specimen in a border. Its ability to survive and thrive has been called "almost weed-like"; it grows quickly and with great gusto, recovering even if its stems are felled by a cold winter or if you completely cut down the shrub in early spring to control its size.

The large, arching canes are somewhat succulent and dressed in attractive gray-green to blue-green foliage. The sweetly scented flowers form impressive clusters and come in many appealing colors. They draw countless butterflies, as the name would indicate, but also plenty of cruising bees. You can always count on this plant for bountiful, long-lasting summer color.

GOOD CHOICES: very dark purple 'Black Knight' is a classic; 'Royal Red' is a gorgeous ruby red; 'Harlequin' has maroon flowers and cream-variegated leaves for extra interest; the Nanho Series are dwarf plants suited to smaller spaces and smaller gardens

California Lilac

***Ceanothus* species and hybrids**

MATURE HEIGHT × WIDTH: 5-10 feet × 5-10 feet
FLOWER COLORS: blue, white
FLOWER SIZE: 1-2 inch clusters
BLOOM TIME: spring
SOIL: fertile, moist, well drained
ZONES: 8-10

Some people in the arid west are from other parts of the country, and springtime brings a nostalgic longing for lilacs. The California lilac is not quite the same, but it makes a lovely substitute and those transplanted gardeners love it. Native to canyons and hillsides, it tends to flower white or blue, but hybridizers have added richer colors, better, longer-lasting flowers, and tidier-looking forms.

The main thing to know about succeeding with this beautiful shrub is that "less is more." Refrain from watering and fertilizing, or the roots may rot and the plant will die. In nature, California lilac grows on well-drained, rocky slopes and probably gets no summer water. Site the shrub far from the sprinklers or hose, or plant it in a large container and leave it be.

GOOD CHOICES: 'Dark Star' has fabulous, cobalt blue flowers; dark, indigo blue 'Julia Phelps' is a prolific bloomer; 'Snowball' is an excellent white

Camellia

Camellia japonica

MATURE HEIGHT × WIDTH: 6-10 feet × 4-7 feet
FLOWER COLORS: red, pink, white
FLOWER SIZE: 3-5 inches
BLOOM TIME: winter to early spring
SOIL: fertile, moist, well drained
ZONES: 7-9

Gardeners in the South and West value these bushy beauties because they start blooming in winter, when color is a welcome sight. The plant itself has a dense profile, with very dark green, shiny leaves. It grows slowly but, unchecked, can become rather large. It makes a fine hedge but also fits into mixed plantings and can be grown in a large container. Because it is shallow-rooted, it should be placed out of the way of foot traffic and receive a protective mulch.

And the flowers! Plush and perfectly formed, they come in many beautiful colors. Beware, however, of cold or excessively wet weather, both of which end the dreamy beauty as unopened buds and petals turn to brown mush. At its peak, however, there is no finer sight than a camellia bush in full and glorious bloom.

GOOD CHOICES: lovely light pink, double 'Debutante'; pristine white 'White Empress'; bold red, later-blooming 'Flame'; for cooler regions there are hardier hybrids between other species that bloom in the late fall, such as 'Winter's Charm' and 'Snow Flurry'

FLOWERING SHRUBS

Daphne
Daphne × burkwoodii
MATURE HEIGHT × WIDTH: 3-4 feet × 4-5 feet
FLOWER COLORS: pink, white
FLOWER SIZE: 2-inch umbels
BLOOM TIME: spring to early summer
SOIL: well drained
ZONES: 5-8

If your garden is small or space is limited, yet you want a flowering shrub with heady fragrance, daphne is a perfect choice. Dense, broad, and mounded in form, it covers itself with the loveliest, sweetly scented flower heads late every spring. These are generally pink, though white forms exist. Fall brings a burst of jaunty little red fruits that look grand against the dark-green leaves. The very popular cultivar 'Carol Mackie' has cream-rimmed leaves that add a touch of elegance.

Daphne thrives in full sun and doesn't like damp soil, so plant it in a well-drained spot and avoid soaking it. A little spring fertilizer improves the flowering. This shrub is also small and compact enough to be shown off in a large tub or planter box, sited on a patio or poolside, where everyone can enjoy it.

GOOD CHOICES: 'Carol Mackie', widely considered the best form, has light pink flowers and variegated leaves on plants 3 feet by 3 feet

Deutzia
Deutzia gracilis
MATURE HEIGHT × WIDTH: 3-6 feet × 3-6 feet
FLOWER COLORS: white, pink
FLOWER SIZE: 1 inch
BLOOM TIME: late spring
SOIL: average, well drained
ZONES: 5-8

An old-fashioned favorite, deutzia makes a lovely sight late every spring with its frothy clusters of snowy white, sometime pink-tinged, flowers. These last for at least two weeks. It makes a gorgeous backdrop for a display of later-blooming tulips or Dutch iris, or let a delicate clematis twine through it. When the flowers fade, prune immediately if you prune at all, for next year's flower buds will soon begin developing and you don't want to clip those off.

The rest of the year, this mounding shrub is clothed in attractive, bright green, toothed leaves. There is a striking variegated-leaved version. Deutzia blends well in a mixed shrub border, particularly with needled evergreens and later blooming species such as viburnum and butterfly bush.

GOOD CHOICES: 'Nikko' is a dwarf version, reaching 1-2 feet tall and up to 5 feet wide, which means you can use it as a low hedge or groundcover; 'Variegata' has yellow-and-green leaves

Flowering Quince
Chaenomeles speciosa
MATURE HEIGHT × WIDTH: 3-6 feet × 6-8 feet
FLOWER COLORS: red, reddish-orange, pink, white
FLOWER SIZE: 1 1/2-2 inches
BLOOM TIME: mid-spring
SOIL: average, well drained
ZONES: 5-9

Among hot-colored flowering shrubs, quince is a standout. It's not difficult to grow, needing only decent soil in sun or part sun (though flowering is better in full sun). The delicate flowers appear in early spring before the leaves, and can be cherry red, tomato red, or even white or pink, depending on the cultivar you choose. They are followed in fall by edible but sharp-tasting fruits that you can leave for the birds or use in jelly.

Be advised that the bushes get dense and twiggy over time, and stem ends have a spiny tip. As such, quince makes a good boundary-marking hedge or street-side planting. And the bright, bold flowers signal the start of spring! Branches can be cut and brought indoors in early spring and forced into bloom.

GOOD CHOICES: 'Texas Scarlet' has abundant orange-red flowers and a more compact habit than the species; 'Cameo' has fluffy, double, peachy-pink flowers; 'Toyo Nishiki' has white, pink, and red flowers all on the same plant

Forsythia
Forsythia × intermedia
MATURE HEIGHT × WIDTH: 2-6 feet × 2-8 feet
FLOWER COLORS: yellow
FLOWER SIZE: 1 inch
BLOOM TIME: early spring
SOIL: well drained
ZONES: 6-9

A landscaper once remarked that there is no point in having a forsythia in your yard if you are going to constantly chop it back. The plant's natural form is lush and sweeping and, given enough space on all sides, it is a glorious fountain of yellow every spring and thick with good green foliage the rest of the season. It makes a fine hedge, not only because of the profuse flowering and dense foliage, but because the stems are so closely packed that even in the winter and bare of leaves, it still blocks your view of the street or your neighbor's yard. Remember to at least clip out old and dead wood to keep the plant handsome and in good health.

Improved, newer forms that aren't as rangy, with more, bigger, and longer-lasting flowers, have superseded the older varieties. So you might consider putting in a plant or two, or replacing old, overgrown ones. For an early bouquet bring cut stems indoors to force them into bloom.

GOOD CHOICES: 'Fiesta' only gets 3 feet high; 'Arnold Dwarf' tops out at 4 feet; 'Northern Gold', out of Canada, is super-hardy and floriferous

FLOWERING SHRUBS

Fothergilla
Fothergilla species
MATURE HEIGHT × WIDTH: 5-10 feet × 5-7 feet
FLOWER COLORS: creamy white
FLOWER SIZE: 2-inch clusters
BLOOM TIME: late spring
SOIL: moist, well drained
ZONES: 5-8

While often praised for its vivid, multi-hued fall foliage show, fothergilla also has a great spring flower display. The entire plant explodes with small bottlebrush-like blossoms (technically, what you see are the stamens, not true petals) of creamy white—very showy and pretty! They waft a spicy, honey scent over your garden.

Multi-stemmed fothergilla is a good-looking plant through the summer months, too. Pests and diseases rarely trouble it and the foliage is a nice medium green. If *Fothergilla major* is just too large for your yard (though bear in mind it does grow slowly), try a dwarf type. This shrub's only requirement is moist, well-drained soil that is somewhat acidic.

GOOD CHOICES: *F. major* is a handsome large shrub; the best dwarf version is *F. gardenii* 'Mt. Airy'

Gardenia
Gardenia augusta (G. jasminoides)
MATURE HEIGHT × WIDTH: 2-8 feet × 2-8 feet
FLOWER COLORS: white
FLOWER SIZE: 1-5 inches
BLOOM TIME: summer
SOIL: fertile, moist, well drained
ZONES: 8-10

Gardeners in the South or West enjoy this beautiful shrub by planting a specimen of it (preferably near the front door or patio or even a full hedge. Everyone else can try it in a container in a sunny spot. It responds well to trimming and shaping, becoming more dense.

The leaves are rich green and lustrous, even on the hottest days. And the flowers are utterly breathtaking: like a loose white rose, but with waxy, more durable petals, and a captivating perfume. Remove faded flowers promptly, and the plant will keep on blooming. It's also wise to provide regular water when the weather is dry to support continuous flower production. Sometimes gardenias have to contend with whiteflies and aphids, but if you see these pests early and blast them off with the hose, the plant should still prosper.

GOOD CHOICES: ever-popular 'Mystery' produces a constant supply of large 5-inch flowers; 'Veitchii' is a compact grower (about 4 feet tall and wide) with plenty of smaller blooms (1-1$^{1}/_{2}$ inches)

FLOWERING SHRUBS

Hebe
Hebe species and hybrids
MATURE HEIGHT × WIDTH: 2-5 feet × 2-5 feet
FLOWER COLORS: purple, blue, red, white
FLOWER SIZE: 3-4 inch spikes
BLOOM TIME: late summer
SOIL: average to poor, well drained
ZONES: 10-11

In mild climates, on patios, city balconies, and in seaside gardens, hebe is a valuable flowering shrub. It's tough and pretty, with plenty of glossy evergreen leaves that are rarely marred by pests, diseases, or environmental stress. It also blooms later in the summer, when color is good to have. The showy flower spikes are generally purple, red, or maroon. It makes a splendid mass planting or hedge, or dependable backdrop for a mixed flower border. It can also be grown in a container in cooler regions and kept indoors over winter in a sunroom. Some forms have variegated foliage also.

GOOD CHOICES: 'Imperialis' has magenta flowers against reddish foliage; 'Coed' has pinkish-purple blooms all summer long

Hydrangea
Hydrangea species and hybrids
MATURE HEIGHT × WIDTH: 3-6 feet × 3-6 feet
FLOWER COLORS: purple, pink, white
FLOWER SIZE: 4-10 inch clusters
BLOOM TIME: summer
SOIL: fertile, moist, well drained
ZONES: 6-9

Generous mophead or broad lacecap flowers billow from these excellent shrubs, and few gardeners can resist! Some new cultivars of *H. macrophylla* will rebloom. The native oakleaf hydrangea, *H. quercifolia*, has pyramidal flower clusters of creamy white; the species form of the native *H. arborescens* has delicate, white, lacecap clusters, though its popular cultivar 'Annabelle' has enormous rounded heads.

The flowers are gorgeous in bouquets, fresh or dried. Some hydrangeas also have colorful fall foliage. One large, graceful hydrangea in the middle of a lawn is a lovely sight, but if you have the space, they also make fine groupings or hedges.

GOOD CHOICES: 'White Swan' is a gorgeous white; 'Forever Pink' is a favorite pink; 'Dooley' is a reblooming blue; 'Nikko Blue' is a bit more cold hardy than the others; of the lacecaps, 'Blue Wave' is an excellent blue and 'Mariesii' is a superb white; *H. quercifolia* 'Snowflake' has panicles 12 to 18 inches long of double blooms; 'Annabelle' remains a popular white-flowered form of *H. arborescens*

Kerria
Kerria japonica
MATURE HEIGHT × WIDTH: 3-5 feet × 4-6 feet
FLOWER COLORS: yellow
FLOWER SIZE: 1-2 inches
BLOOM TIME: spring into summer
SOIL: average, well drained
ZONES: 4-9

Like plush little yellow roses, the abundant flowers of kerria always charm. (As it turns out, kerria is in the rose family, so the similarity is not a coincidence.) They appear in great numbers at the ends of stems, completely covering the bush. Their first big flush is in late spring, but more appear on and off throughout the summer months or in the fall. Fall also brings golden-yellow leaves.

Not a fussy plant, kerria adapts to most soils and appreciates a little shade, more in areas where the summers are blazingly hot. With age, it takes on a dense, broad, rounded form, so it's nice to use in a hedge or as a backdrop shrub.

GOOD CHOICES: 'Pleniflora' has flowers like small yellow balls, and grows bigger and wider than the species; 'Aureo-Marginata' has the bonus of yellow-variegated leaves

Lilac
Syringa vulgaris
MATURE HEIGHT × WIDTH: 4-10 feet × 4-10 feet
FLOWER COLORS: purple, pink, white
FLOWER SIZE: 6-10 inch clusters
BLOOM TIME: late spring
SOIL: fertile, moist, well drained
ZONES: 4-8

What would springtime be without the heady, nostalgic fragrance of lilac blooms drifting across the yard? The old, large, rangy lilacs that are so prone to powdery mildew on their leaves have become a thing of the past; many excellent newer varieties are on the market these days and you should choose from among them, whether you are installing your own first lilac or replacing one that has fallen out of favor.

Flower color has also seen dramatic improvements. The purples are richer, the pinks brighter, the whites crisper—and all hues are longer lasting, in the garden or a vase. The one thing plant breeders could never improve upon is the scent, and no matter which new cultivar you may choose, you'll still have that to delight in.

GOOD CHOICES: 'Tinkerbelle' has wine-red buds that open to pink flowers, plus mildew-resistant foliage; 'Katherine Havemeyer' has purple buds that open to double, lavender-pink blossoms and is also mildew resistant; unusual 'Sensation' has white-rimmed, purple flowers

Mock Orange
Philadelphus coronarius
MATURE HEIGHT × WIDTH: 5-8 feet × 4-7 feet
FLOWER COLORS: white
FLOWER SIZE: 1-2 inches
BLOOM TIME: early summer
SOIL: average, well drained
ZONES: 5-8

Mountain Laurel
Kalmia latifolia
MATURE HEIGHT × WIDTH: 5-8 feet × 5-8 feet
FLOWER COLORS: white, red, pink, bicolors
FLOWER SIZE: 6-inch clusters
BLOOM TIME: spring
SOIL: moist, well drained
ZONES: 5-8

An old-fashioned favorite, mock orange has a loose, casual profile and can become a rather big plant. Early every summer, it sparkles with numerous fragrant flower clusters; the flowers of some forms are single and some are double. The cultivars are much more productive than the species.

As far as siting goes, your best bet is to plant one in an informal part of the yard, in sun or light shade. Just be sure you'll be in range of that delicious fragrance when early summer comes—why not right outside the kitchen window, or off the side of the deck? Mock orange can be pruned directly after flowering, or, if warranted, cut down completely to the base for a fresh start next year.

GOOD CHOICES: 'Nanus' is a nice smaller edition, topping out at 4 feet; 'Variegatus' has cream-bordered leaves; 'Minnesota Snowflake' is tall, bushy, and very hardy in cold climates

Hailing originally from the woodlands of New England and Appalachia, this cousin of azaleas and rhododendrons has magnificent flower clusters, which foam forth every spring. These now come in many appealing hues. Closer inspection reveals that individual flowers are banded, blotched, or freckled with a contrasting color.

Mountain laurel does best when you can give it a spot with moist but well-drained, slightly acidic soil that is organically rich, and in dappled shade, such as in a shrub border or foundation planting. However, it will also grow well in partial or full sun, so long as the soil is kept moist with regular watering and protective mulch around the roots.

GOOD CHOICES: 'Carousel' has bright pink buds that burst open to reveal intricate starburst patterns on the inside, in cinnamon-purple; 'Olympic Fire' has bright red buds that open large and pink; 'Snowdrift' is a superior white; soft-pink-flowered 'Tiddlywinks' and pink-and-white 'Elf' are dwarf forms

FLOWERING SHRUBS

Pearlbush
Exochorda × macrantha
MATURE HEIGHT × WIDTH: 4 feet × 7 feet
FLOWER COLORS: white
FLOWER SIZE: ¹/₂-1 inch
BLOOM TIME: spring
SOIL: well drained
ZONES: 5-9

There are other pearlbushes, but they are typically too big for the average garden. This hybrid is the best of the lot, with a more compact, refined growth habit. The flowering every spring is astounding—the plant seems to billow with white blooms. It makes a spectacular backdrop for a tulip or daffodil display. The name comes from the fact that the buds, prior to opening, look like strings of pearls.

Out of bloom, it is a rather plain but undemanding shrub with a fountain-like profile. The green leaves are whitish below, which adds some appeal. Pearlbush is never any trouble, adapting well to most soils and sun or part shade. Prune to encourage it to grow bushier; left to its own devices, it can get leggy.

GOOD CHOICES: 'The Bride' is an excellent smaller edition, topping out at 3 to 4 feet tall

Plumbago
Plumbago auriculata (P. capensis)
MATURE HEIGHT × WIDTH: 6 feet × 8-10 feet
FLOWER COLORS: blue, lavender, white
FLOWER SIZE: 1 inch
BLOOM TIME: summer
SOIL: average to dry, well drained
ZONES: 9-10

For gardeners in hot, frost-free climates, this sprawling, mounding shrub is a boon. Not only does it tolerate the average to dry soils, lack of rainfall, and hot sun, it does so with amazing pluck. The small leaves, light to medium green, always look fresh. And the flowers, which are especially durable and long lasting, cluster at the stem ends in shades of blue, lavender, or white. (They resemble the funnel-form flowers of phlox.)

New plants get off to a slow start, but in ensuing years, hold their own and even recover well from exposure to an occasional unexpected frost. Plumbago is a nice hedge plant, looks pretty along a fence or wall, and is a fine backdrop for a flower garden. Some people get a skin rash after pruning and shaping, so wear garden gloves as a precaution.

GOOD CHOICES: the species is pale blue; 'Alba' is a good white-flowered selection

Potentilla
Potentilla fruticosa
MATURE HEIGHT × WIDTH: 3-4 feet × 3-4 feet
FLOWER COLORS: yellow, orange, white, red, pink
FLOWER SIZE: 1-2 inches
BLOOM TIME: midsummer to fall
SOIL: well drained
ZONES: 2-7

This compact shrub is very free-flowering. It starts bloom-ing in the middle of the summer, and remains alive with color well into fall. No pests or diseases ever trouble it, nor does it require much in the way of pruning or fussing. And all it wants is a sunny spot in decent, well-drained soil.

Owing to its medium size and dense growth, potentilla, or bush cinquefoil, is useful as a hedge plant or as a color-ful part of a shrub border. Individual plants, however, can do much to brighten up a mixed flower border where there's not much color in the latter part of the growing season. If yellow isn't what you want, check out the various cultivars.

GOOD CHOICES: 'Abbotswood' has nice, larger white flowers; aptly named 'Tangerine' brings a touch of orange; 'Red Ace' is a highly touted red flower with a yellow center, but it can fade in hot summers; if you still want yellow, try 'Gold Drop' or 'Goldfinger'

Rhododendron
Rhododendron species and hybrids
MATURE HEIGHT × WIDTH: 3-6 feet × 3-6 feet
FLOWER COLORS: red, white, pink, purple
FLOWER SIZE: 2-5 inches
BLOOM TIME: mid- to late spring
SOIL: fertile, slightly acidic, well drained
ZONES: 4-8

Flower-lovers lavish affection on rhododendrons. Though their moments of springtime glory in our gardens are all too fleeting, these stately shrubs are completely worth it. If the only rhododendrons you are familiar with are the ubiqui-tous mauve or purple ones, explore the many other flower colors, and you may succumb to their charms. Abundant trusses of bell-shaped flowers appear in spring, glowing against the backdrop of their large, evergreen leaves. Rhodo-dendrons need dappled shade and moist but well-drained soil that is slightly acidic. If your soil is a bit on the heavy side you might need to plant this shrub high and thickly mulched, or in a raised bed. Nice in a woodland or shaded wildflower garden, rhodies are also lovely in a formal setting.

GOOD CHOICES: the gorgeous, apple-blossom-hued flower clusters of *R. yakusimanum* are breathtaking; 'Cunning-ham's White', a *R. catawbiense* cultivar, is a glorious lime-dusted white; the ruby-red, frilly flowers of 'Hellikki' are ravishing

FLOWERING SHRUBS

Rock Rose
Cistus species
MATURE HEIGHT × WIDTH: 2-5 feet × 2-5 feet
FLOWER COLORS: many
FLOWER SIZE: 2-4 inches
BLOOM TIME: spring to summer
SOIL: well drained
ZONES: 8-10

Justly popular in mild climates for their showy, dependable flowers, rock roses are fast-growing sun-lovers. They are also tough, tolerating wind, salt spray, drought, and heat. Through it all, the gray-green, crinkly foliage remains good-looking. Their pretty crepe-paper petals and single form almost remind you of poppy blooms, though they are smaller, and they come in an array of appealing hues, from white to pink and red to purple, often with contrasting or blotched centers.

Rock roses mingle well with other drought-tolerant plants, remaining in bloom for many weeks, and may also be used to cover a dry bank or curb strip, where they help control erosion. Truly "a diamond in the rough"!

GOOD CHOICES: *C. purpureus* has reddish-purple flowers with a red spot at the base of each petal; *C. ladanifer* has white flowers with dark crimson spots

Rose
Rosa species and hybrids
MATURE HEIGHT × WIDTH: 2-6 feet × 2-6 feet
FLOWER COLORS: pink, red, white, yellow, orange
FLOWER SIZE: 1-4 inches
BLOOM TIME: late spring through summer
SOIL: fertile, well drained
ZONES: 4-9

Quite possibly, no other flowering shrub is as beautiful or as long blooming as the rose. It comes in an amazing array of flower colors and forms, from one-to-a-stem hybrid teas with their vase-shaped profiles, to bushy, multi-flowered floribundas; to tough and hardy shrub roses; to the plush-flowered, fragrant, long-blooming English roses. There is surely a rose for every gardener and every garden!

One major plus of roses is the flowers of some types can continue for most of the summer. Careful selection, good care, and deadheading (or bouquet-cutting) help maximize this important feature. If pests or diseases are an issue in your area, make a point of purchasing varieties that are known to be resistant, and then giving them good care so they stay in good health.

GOOD CHOICES: newer varieties, such as 'Knock Out', 'Cherry Parfait', 'Hot Cocoa', and 'Gemini', tend to be more floriferous and disease-resistant; older varieties that are still prospering, such as 'The Fairy' and 'Iceberg', have obviously stood the test of time

Rose-of-Sharon
Hibiscus syriacus
MATURE HEIGHT × WIDTH: 6-10 feet × 4-6 feet
FLOWER COLORS: pink, red, purple, white, bicolors
FLOWER SIZE: 3-5 inches
BLOOM TIME: mid- to late summer
SOIL: average to moist, well drained
ZONES: 5-9

Spirea
Spiraea species and hybrids
MATURE HEIGHT × WIDTH: 2-6 feet × 3-8 feet
FLOWER COLORS: white, pink
FLOWER SIZE: 2-3 inch clusters
BLOOM TIME: spring into summer
SOIL: average, well drained
ZONES: 4-9

This long-flowering, upright-growing shrub has long been a favorite because the colorful blossoms appear around midsummer, when most other flowering shrubs have passed their peak. They look just like hibiscus blooms, though smaller.

Rose-of-Sharon plants make good solo plantings, provided you can give them enough space all around to let them achieve their mature spread and shape. They're less successful as hedges because trimming and pruning to keep them in bounds reduces flowering. Moist, fertile soil helps them thrive and extra water in dry spells is a must.

GOOD CHOICES: 'Red Heart', given an Royal Horticultural Society Award of Merit, has single, crisp white blooms centered with dark red; 'Jeanne d'Arc' is the best double white; 'Minerva' has pretty pink-tinged lavender flowers with ruby red centers, up to 5 inches across, and is especially long-blooming; 'Blue Bird' is sky blue with a wine-colored eye

There are numerous species, cultivars, and hybrids of spirea, with white or pink flowers, and leaves of various shades of green, from lime-green to blue-green. Some are tall and cascading like bridal wreath spirea, while others form mounds of delicate flower clusters and small foliage on wiry stems.

To prosper, all spireas need are a spot in full sun and ample elbowroom to reach their mature size. Unless it's a very dry year, normal rainfall is all an established plant will need. If you do feel like shaping or pruning, do so immediately after flowering since the branches will soon start developing buds for the next year; pruning or shearing will also generate a flush of fresh foliage (especially nice on the chartreuse-leaved forms).

GOOD CHOICES: 'Shirobana' has white and pink flowers on the same plant; 'Limemound' has bright pink flowers and chartreuse leaves; 'Plena' is a double-flowered version of bridal wreath

St. John's Wort
Hypericum species and hybrids
MATURE HEIGHT × WIDTH: 3 feet × 3 feet
FLOWER COLORS: yellow
FLOWER SIZE: 2 inches
BLOOM TIME: summer
SOIL: average, well drained
ZONES: 6-8

Small, bright, waxy-textured, golden yellow flowers stud these dense, low-growing bushes in summer. The plants are slow growing and never very large or sprawling, and they do well in average to poor soil, even dry, heavy ground, where few other plants prosper. They are very popular with bees and other pollinators.

The blue-green leaves grow thickly and are a good backdrop for the luxurious showing of bright flowers. Probably the best use of this plant is massed or grouped, to get the best impact. Note that it is not the plant with medicinal uses, which is its cousin *H. perforatum*. Actually, all plant parts of this St. John's wort are poisonous.

GOOD CHOICES: *H. frondosum* 'Sunburst' is considered the best, for it stays compact and flowers profusely; related *H. kalmianum* 'Ames' is much more cold hardy than the species (to Zone 4) and has especially blue-green foliage

Sweet Pepperbush
Clethra alnifolia
MATURE HEIGHT × WIDTH: 5-10 feet × 4-6 feet
FLOWER COLORS: white, pink
FLOWER SIZE: 4-6 inch spikes
BLOOM TIME: mid- to late summer
SOIL: moist, well drained
ZONES: 4-8

Spicy, sweet fragrance drifts on the midsummer breeze from this handsome native shrub, prompting your garden visitors to go hunting for its source. It emanates from plush spikes of white or pale pink, which cover the plant and last for up to a month. Few other shrubs are in bloom at this time, which makes sweet pepperbush all the more enchanting. Dark peppercorn-like fruit capsules follow in fall and look great against the orange-yellow fall foliage.

In nature, it likes damp ground, so if you have a pond or moist-ground area on your property, sweet pepperbush will thrive. Alternatively, just make sure you keep it well watered. It also prefers slightly acidic soil. Pests and diseases rarely trouble it.

GOOD CHOICES: 'Rosea' has glossier foliage than the species and light pink buds that open pale pink and gradually turn white; old favorite 'Paniculata' has bigger flowers on a more vigorous plant

Viburnum
Viburnum species and hybrids
MATURE HEIGHT × WIDTH: 5-9 feet × 5-9 feet
FLOWER COLORS: white, pink
FLOWER SIZE: 3-6 inch clusters
BLOOM TIME: mid- to late spring
SOIL: average to moist, well drained
ZONES: 3-8

Viburnums are easy and trouble-free, and they have beauty to offer in every season. The flowers are crisp and white (sometimes pink), in flat clusters or balls; often they are spicily scented. The dark-green, textured foliage is quite good looking. Fall brings attractive red, black, blue, or yellow berries and colorful foliage.

Viburnums tend to be shallow-rooted, so you should not site a plant in the path of foot traffic, and should apply a protective mulch. Pruning is rarely needed, though you can thin dense plants by trimming off branches at the base or trunk.

GOOD CHOICES: *V. plicatum* var. *tomentosum*, a big plant with spreading, horizontal branches, has two excellent cultivars—'Shasta', with lacy flowers up to 6 inches across, and 'Mariseii', with especially fragrant flowers; *V. × burkwoodii* is outstanding in the Midwest and South; the cultivar 'Mohawk' has brilliant red buds that open to scented white balls, plus excellent fall foliage; *V. dentatum* 'Blue Muffin' is a compact, 3- to 5-foot variety with flattened flower heads

Weigela
Weigela florida
MATURE HEIGHT × WIDTH: 3-6 feet × 4-6 feet
FLOWER COLORS: red, purple, pink
FLOWER SIZE: 1 inch
BLOOM TIME: late spring
SOIL: average, well drained
ZONES: 4-8

Thanks to its profuse tubular red-hued flowers, this sentimental-favorite informal shrub draws hummingbirds. It also has the ability to shrug off pests and diseases, tolerate pollution, and adapt to a variety of soil types (except the most wet or dry) and exposures (except full shade). The foliage of some cultivars is also attractive, variegated cream and green, or wine-tinged.

Because the arching branches naturally spill outward, you need to give this plant enough room. The tips may get winterkilled, and you may have to do some shaping, but otherwise let the plant be its luxurious, exuberant self.

GOOD CHOICES: 'Wine & Roses' has dark purple foliage that makes a stunning contrast with its rosy-pink flowers; 'Red Prince' sports plenty of non-fading red blooms; 'Variegata' has splashy, cream-variegated leaves

Small Flowering Trees

trees may be on your property for shade, privacy, boundary definition, or some other practical reason. But to grow a tree for its
ornamental value is a different sort of matter. This is a decision to
acquire a tree solely for its beauty. A smaller-size one is meant to be a
garden element, a plant to be enjoyed and cherished. It might get a
place of honor in the middle of an expanse of lawn, it might flank your
home's entrance or the garden gate, or it might be happiest tucked into
a sheltering corner where you have to take a little stroll out through
the yard to enjoy it.

Because this is not a decision you make every day and the plant
will be long lived, it behooves you to give it careful thought. The goal
is a smaller-size tree with appealing flowers. Plenty of trees have attractive or intriguing growth habits, beautiful or edible fruit, glorious fall
foliage, even handsome bark. But a tree chosen first and foremost for
its flowers (though it may have some or all of those other desirable qualities) is a great joy. Its annual flowering is an event!

Chaste Tree
Vitex angus-castus
MATURE HEIGHT × WIDTH: 8-20 × 4-8 feet
FLOWER COLORS: purple, pink, white
FLOWER SIZE: 5-8 inch racemes
BLOOM TIME: summer
SOIL: fertile, moist, well drained
ZONES: 6-8

An attractive, large multi-stemmed shrub or rounded small tree (depending on how you prune it), chaste tree has a lot to recommend it. Aromatic fan-shaped leaves made of slender gray-green leaflets, silvery on the undersides, are always handsome. They're joined in midsummer by plenty of lavender-violet flowers in clusters, slightly reminiscent of butterfly bush or lilac. It's a pretty, and welcome, sight at that time of the year—and, happily, the blooms tend to last until fall. (In the winter months, you can admire the chunky, corky-looking bark.) This is not a cold-hardy plant, and performs best in the hot South and West. It can be cut back close to the ground every spring to control its size in the flower border.

GOOD CHOICES: the species is an outstanding blue; 'Shoal Creek' has flower clusters 12 to 18 inches long; the forma *alba* has white flowers; 'Rosea' has pink

Crabapple
Malus species and hybrids
MATURE HEIGHT × WIDTH: 6-30 × 6-20 feet
FLOWER COLORS: pink, white, red
FLOWER SIZE: $1/2$-1 inch
BLOOM TIME: spring
SOIL: average, well drained
ZONES: 5-8

It's no wonder so many people grow the crabapple as an ornamental tree, either in a prominent spot or in rows or groupings—it has so much to offer. The springtime flower show is always beautiful and often sweetly fragrant. The leaves that follow are a good dark green or sometimes appealing shades of purple or wine-red. Fall brings a flurry of ornamental fruit in red, purple, or yellow—sometimes the birds eat these, or you can harvest them for a tart jelly.

Decent, well-drained soil is best, although crabapples will adjust to life in rocky ground and slightly acid or slightly alkaline conditions. They tolerate heat well. All in all, this old favorite is a champ.

GOOD CHOICES: white-flowered 'Donald Wyman' is an excellent, long-time favorite in many areas; 'Liset' has beautiful, dark purple-pink blossoms; 'Royalty' is a picture in red, with wine-red leaves, crimson flowers, and dark red fruit

SMALL FLOWERING TREES

Crape Myrtle
Lagerstroemia indica
MATURE HEIGHT × WIDTH: 10-20 feet × 5-10 feet
FLOWER COLORS: pink, purple, red, white
FLOWER SIZE: 8-10 inch clusters
BLOOM TIME: summer to fall
SOIL: well drained
ZONES: 6-10

A common sight in the South and popular in other hot, sunny areas, crape myrtle is truly a can't-miss flowering shrub. A single plant is a terrific specimen, while smaller or pruned-down ones make very good hedges or screens. The beautiful bark, if you allow it to be visible, is smooth, gray, and exfoliating to create a multicolored look; some types have cinnamon colored bark. And the leaves, at maturity, are a tidy, shiny green—and often put on a vivid show of yellow, orange, or red in the fall. But the fabulous flowers are the main reason to grow crape myrtles, and these days there are more and better choices than ever, as a trip to a good local nursery will show! As soon as the first flush of flowers fades, cut them off and wait a few weeks for an encore.

GOOD CHOICES: coral-pink 'Comanche'; 'Seminole' is vivid pink; dark-red 'Victor' is an excellent dwarf variety, topping out at 3 feet high; 'Dynamite' is a striking red with reddish tinted new foliage

Dogwood
Cornus florida
MATURE HEIGHT × WIDTH: 10-25 feet × 10-25 feet
FLOWER COLORS: white, pink
FLOWER SIZE: 2-4 inches
BLOOM TIME: spring
SOIL: fertile, moist, well drained
ZONES: 5-9

Recent years of anthracnose disease and borers have put a damper on the long-held public enthusiasm for this excellent ornamental tree, though anthracnose is typically only a problem in high altitudes. Nowadays if you want to add a small dogwood tree to your landscape, you should shop for one of the newer varieties that are clearly billed as resistant. The Stellar Series offered by some nurseries is good. Or look to the Kousa dogwood, *C. kousa*, which has more star-shaped blooms and flowers a little later (after the foliage has emerged). Though often planted in the middle of a lawn, the trees are vulnerable to weed killers present in some lawn-grass fertilizers.

GOOD CHOICES: 'Stellar Pink' is a disease-resistant hybrid with bright pink flowers; those of similar 'Aurora' are white; 'Alba Plena' has double white, almost gardenia-like flowers; 'Red Pygmy' is a novelty—a red-flowered dwarf, suitable for smaller garden spaces

154

Flowering Cherry
Prunus serrulata

MATURE HEIGHT × WIDTH: 20-25 feet × 10-15 feet
FLOWER COLORS: white, pink
FLOWER SIZE: 1-2 inches
BLOOM TIME: spring
SOIL: well drained
ZONES: 5-8

Among smaller-size ornamental trees, Japanese flowering cherry is deservedly a classic. It has an attractive horizontal spreading habit and is cloaked in the most beautiful flowers for a couple of weeks every spring. It's fun to clip off a few branches just as blooming is starting and put them in a vase indoors to open. The tree maintains good-looking leaves through the summer and into the fall, when the foliage turns a stylish bronze or red.

The key to a great flower display is positioning the tree in full sun in soil that drains well; soggy ground is debilitating, and exposure to drying winds can also compromise performance. Flowering cherries can be included in larger mixed borders, or as a centerpiece in a formal garden, and they don't mind if you plant flowers at their feet.

GOOD CHOICES: 'Kwanzan' has splendid double pink blossoms; 'Mount Fuji' ('Shirotae') has pink buds that open to white, fragrant, semi-double blossoms

Fringe Tree
Chionanthus virginicus

MATURE HEIGHT × WIDTH: 12-20 feet × 12-20 feet
FLOWER COLORS: white
FLOWER SIZE: 1 inch
BLOOM TIME: late spring to early summer
SOIL: moist, well-drained
ZONES: 3-9

Beloved for its elegant beauty, broadly spreading habit, and scented flowers, this native American plant is found along stream banks and the borders of swamps and thus performs best in cultivation when it gets sufficient soil moisture. Other than that, it is no trouble at all to grow well.

Late every spring, for several weeks, the tree is spangled with clusters of slender, silky white flowers. En masse, they look fleecy and fringe-like, hence the common name. These waft a sweet, honey-like fragrance.

Summer foliage is dark green. Clusters of tiny, dark, blue, olive-like fruits dangle against yellow foliage in autumn. Fringe tree is dioecious, meaning it has separate male and female trees: to get the fruit you must have both.

GOOD CHOICES: the typical native species form is outstanding; *C. pygmaeus* is an endangered species native to Florida that is dwarf, between 4 and 6 feet tall (more like a big shrub); *C. retusus*, Chinese fringe tree, has smaller, glossier leaves

SMALL FLOWERING TREES

Golden Chain Tree
Laburnum × watereri

MATURE HEIGHT × WIDTH: 12-15 feet × 10 feet
FLOWER COLORS: yellow
FLOWER SIZE: 1-2 inches
BLOOM TIME: late spring
SOIL: moist, well drained
ZONES: 5-7

We can all dream of traipsing the famous Laburnum Walk at Bodnant Gardens in Wales, a supporting archway about 75 yards long with these trees trained over it, the long flower clusters draping their glory down all around like an extravagant golden wisteria. But you can certainly still enjoy this fantastic small tree in many parts of the country. It is not heat tolerant and doesn't like soggy soil, but otherwise adapts well to a protected spot in full sun or partial shade. Out of bloom, it is a nice, unremarkable tree of bright-green leaves with a slight bluish tinge; fall color is negligible. But the flowers that appear in late spring are spectacular. Seedpods follow and should be removed and disposed of, as they not only sap energy from the tree but are poisonous. Perhaps you can't fit in your own "Walk," but you could place one or more plants close to the house or by a street-side fence.

GOOD CHOICES: graceful 'Vossii' has sensational racemes of blossoms up to 2 feet long

Magnolia
Magnolia species and hybrids

MATURE HEIGHT × WIDTH: 10-25 feet × 10-25 feet
FLOWER COLORS: pink, white, yellow
FLOWER SIZE: 5-12 inches
BLOOM TIME: mid- to late spring, summer
SOIL: fertile, moist, well drained
ZONES: 5–8

There is true love, and true heartbreak, among fans of the gorgeous and prolific-flowering magnolia. For although the heavenly scented, chalice-shaped blossoms are wonderful, a spring frost can ruin the long-awaited show by killing the flower buds on some types, notably *M.* × *soulangiana* and *M. stellata*. Find a type that will not be vulnerable to the climate in your area.

Take a look at the predicted ultimate size of the tree you want. Magnolias can grow tall as well as broad, particularly the native species, and you want to choose one that will fit where you intend to place it.

GOOD CHOICES: cold-hardy, evergreen *M. grandiflora* 'Edith Bogue' has a neat, pyramidal form and excellent perfumed white flowers; the native *M. acuminata* and its hybrids and cultivars are also hardier up North ('Miss Honeybee', 'Butterflies', and 'Elizabeth' all have creamy yellow flowers); *M. liliiflora* offers many cultivars of smaller stature for smaller gardens

Oleander
Nerium oleander
MATURE HEIGHT × WIDTH: 3-12 feet × 3-12 feet
FLOWER COLORS: white, pink, red, lavender, yellow
FLOWER SIZE: 2-3 inches
BLOOM TIME: summer
SOIL: average to poor, well drained
ZONES: 8-9

Justly popular where it can be grown, oleander has proven itself to be a very durable, tough shrub with a wonderfully long bloom season. Thus, it behooves the homeowner to choose a flower color wisely, as it may set the tone for your garden. Luckily, the pretty flowers, which cluster at twig ends, come in all sorts of colors and can be single or double-form. They're also sweetly scented.

Oleanders are easy because they tolerate almost any soil and the abuse of drought, hot sun, pollution, and even soil with high salt content. But this doesn't mean you should neglect care. They'll look much better if you prune early each spring to control size and to shape the shrub. Get rid of spent flowers and leaves, which are not only unsightly, but also poisonous—which is why deer never nibble oleander.

GOOD CHOICES: if you want a big plant for a hedge or screen planting, try white-flowered 'Sister Agnes'; the Petite Series, available in shades of pink, are about 4 feet high; the flowers of 'Ruby Lace' are bright red

Redbud
Cercis canadensis
MATURE HEIGHT × WIDTH: 10-30 × 10-30 feet
FLOWER COLORS: pink, white
FLOWER SIZE: 1/2 inch
BLOOM TIME: spring
SOIL: well drained
ZONES: 4-8

An easy-going small tree, redbud is rather neat and elegant, with gracefully ascending, tiered branches. So it's a nice choice for a suburban yard as a specimen plant or as part of a mixed border.

The lovely flowers appear first on spring's bare branches, maroon in bud and rosy-pink when open. They have good timing, appearing after the earlier-flowering fruit trees (peach, plum) but before the crabapples and late-flowering cherries. After the flowers go by, the heart-shaped leaves emerge, reddish-purple, though they eventually change to shiny green by summer. Regular food and water keep your redbud healthy and beautiful.

GOOD CHOICES: purple leaves and rose-purple flowers decorate 'Forest Pansy'; 'Covey' is a sought-after weeping form with lavender flowers; magenta-flowered *C. occidentalis* is a good, drought-tolerant species for the West

Vines and Climbers

It seems a shame, but installing a flowering vine or climber often seems to be the last thing to occur to us when we are contemplating a new garden or improving the one we have. Perennials and annuals, especially, clamor for open ground and attention. Even at your local garden center, the selection of climbers is almost always miniscule compared to all the other plants. And yet, the inclusion of even one beautiful climber can alter a garden dramatically.

Vertical space is the province of vines and climbers, and when you use them to decorate this dimension, something changes. You can use a surface already present, such as a wall of your house or an outbuilding. You can decorate an otherwise plain or unsightly fence. You can even create vertical planting areas by erecting a trellis or other support, or rigging string from one spot to another or from the bottom of your porch to the top. But when you plant, nurture, and succeed with a flowering vine, your yard feels cozier, more enclosed, more finished…more intimate. Most of all, it looks and feels so much more "planted," so much more colorful. It fulfills its potential as a garden.

While there are many worthy vines to choose from, if you want color, you probably want one of the ones listed here. These plants have proven their ability to grow easily and well, and to bloom generously. Take note that some are annuals, and will need to be replanted each year.

Black-Eyed Susan Vine
Thunbergia alata
MATURE LENGTH: 8 feet
FLOWER COLORS: orange, yellow, white
FLOWER SIZE: 1-1 1/2 inches
BLOOM TIME: summer
SOIL: moist, well drained
ZONES: 9-10

Everyone who sees this flowering vine in your yard will exclaim over it. Once it's going full blast by midsummer, it truly is a spectacle. The medium-green leaves, abetted by twining stems, mount a supporting wire, string, or trellis with ease and form a good backdrop for the sensational flowers. These superficially resemble the popular perennial flower black-eyed Susan, because they have golden petals and dark centers, though they are not actually daisies. Instead, they're broadly flaring trumpets.

There are other ways to show off this great vine: in pots on the stump of a tree, in hanging baskets, or trained over a fence. Just remember, it does best with plenty of sunshine. It is most often grown as an annual, and can be mixed with perennial vines such as clematis or coral honeysuckle, or other annual vines such as morning glory for a lively display.

GOOD CHOICES: 'Alba' is the white version; 'Suzie' has orange-yellow flowers

Clematis
Clematis species and hybrids
MATURE LENGTH: 6-10 feet
FLOWER COLORS: pink, purple, white, red, yellow
FLOWER SIZE: 3-9 inches
BLOOM TIME: late spring, summer, some repeat in fall
SOIL: fertile, moist, well drained, alkaline
ZONES: 4-10

Often referred to as "the Queen of the Climbers," clematis has flowers which seem to come in practically every color of the rainbow. Some forms are double or have accenting ruffs in the center. Different varieties have differing bloom times and pruning requirements.

To get the flower show you've been dreaming of, here are a few tips. First, plant your young vine with its head in the sun and its feet in the shade (create shade by planting a protective nearby skirt of annuals or perennials, and be sure to mulch). Next, be patient. A clematis plant's first year tends to be devoted to growth you can't see, that is, root growth. The big payoff will come the following and subsequent years. Finally, put a support in place early so you don't forget, or end up harming that valuable root system.

GOOD CHOICES: the best whites, always popular, are 'Henryi' and the double 'Duchess of Edinburgh'; 'Nelly Moser' has light and hot pink stripes for a peppermint-candy effect; 'Niobe' is a fantastic ruby red; 'General Sikorski' has brilliant blue blooms with a hint of red in the center

VINES AND CLIMBERS

Climbing Rose
Rosa species and hybrids
MATURE LENGTH: 10-20 feet
FLOWER COLORS: yellow, pink, white, red, purple
FLOWER SIZE: 3-6 inches
BLOOM TIME: summer
SOIL: fertile, moist, well drained
ZONES: 4-9

Nothing can compare with a climbing rose on a summer's day. Bright sunshine inspires lush blooming and maximum fragrance, as the canes drape over a fence, archway, or trellis. Unlike other vines, however, they have no natural way to attach to whatever they are climbing. The long, pliable, often thorny canes need guidance. To avoid abrading the stems with wire or string, try slender pieces of soft rags. Because climbing roses generally remain in bloom all summer, pick your color with care so it doesn't clash with other nearby bloomers.

GOOD CHOICES: cluster-blooming red 'Blaze' is an old favorite; 1999 AAS winner 'Fourth of July' has apple-scented blooms that are vividly striped red and white; peach-scented, soft pink 'New Dawn' is luscious; 1964 Bagatelle Gold Medal winner 'Joseph's Coat' has amazing, multi-hued hot pink/orange/yellow/red blooms; old fashioned, plush-petaled, richly fragrant white 'Sombreuil' is a beauty; for cold climates, bright pink 'William Baffin' is excellent

Honeysuckle
Lonicera × *heckrottii*
MATURE LENGTH: 10-20 feet
FLOWER COLORS: crimson and yellow
FLOWER SIZE: 1½ inches
BLOOM TIME: mid- to late spring
SOIL: average, well drained
ZONES: 6-9

Striking, softly scented bicolor flowers decorate this beloved climber. The buds are crimson but burst open to reveal a sunny yellow interior. The vine sparkles with these blooms for a long spell in springtime, then provides occasional encores on and off throughout the summer. Moist soil, or at least regular watering, helps prolong the blooming.

Honeysuckle vines can grow almost anywhere and you have to be careful or they will take over. Still, eager growth can be a good thing if it is your wish to envelope a trellis, fence, arch, pergola, porch, or shed. You can even let it ramble as a fragrant groundcover. It probably goes without saying, then, that you don't need to fertilize honeysuckle—and you can control its bulk and direction with your clippers.

GOOD CHOICES: vigorous 'Goldflame' has somewhat bigger, brighter flowers

Jasmine
Jasminum officinale
MATURE LENGTH: 10-30 feet
FLOWER COLORS: white
FLOWER SIZE: 1 inch
BLOOM TIME: summer
SOIL: average, well drained
ZONES: 8-10

There are other jasmines worth growing, but this one is excellent and easy to find. It's a twining vine with semi-evergreen leaves and abundant, scented, long-lasting white flowers. Just a whiff of it can make you swoon, or bring back memories of Grandmother's perfume. Regular watering is important to maintain and prolong the flowers.

Jasmine has twining stems, but it may need a little help from guide wires to stay on a support. Or let it drape over a fence or wall. Control growth while creating a denser plant by pinching back rampant stems and pruning annually in autumn or early winter. Alternatively, grow jasmine in a pot or tub: It may be easier to maintain and you can place it where you will enjoy it daily. Containers are the way to go in colder climates.

GOOD CHOICES: 'Affine' has larger, pink-tinged flowers; Spanish jasmine (*J. grandiflorum*) is a shorter vine, between 10 and 15 feet, and has somewhat larger flowers

Moonflower
Ipomoea alba
MATURE LENGTH: 15-40 feet
FLOWER COLORS: white
FLOWER SIZE: 5-6 inches
BLOOM TIME: summer
SOIL: average to moist, well drained
ZONES: 8-10

If you're at work all day, imagine coming home in the evening to see these morning-glory relatives unfurl their big, glowing, satiny white blossoms while radiating their rich, haunting perfume. And the show continues all summer long! The flowers always draw admirers (including night-flying moths).

Fortunately, this breathtaking climber is quite easy to grow. If you live in a cold climate, it's wise to start seeds indoors early (nick or soak the seeds to speed germination) and transplant the seedlings outside after danger of frost is past. If you live in a mild climate, just sow the seeds where you want the vine to grow, and remember to set out a support at that time. Otherwise, the vine will take off across the ground and become tangled.

GOOD CHOICES: the species is the most commonly available, but if you can find it, 'Giant White' lives up to its name with 6-inch blooms

VINES AND CLIMBERS

Morning Glory
Ipomoea tricolor
MATURE LENGTH: 10-12 feet
FLOWER COLORS: blue, red, white, purple, bicolors
FLOWER SIZE: 3-5 inches
BLOOM TIME: summer
SOIL: average, well drained
ZONES: 8-10

These annual vines are simple to grow and bloom heavily throughout the summer. They get their name from the fact that they unfurl their jaunty blossoms in the morning and close by afternoon (they stay open longer on cloudy days). Though usually seen in blue, you can now find morning glory in a whole array of wonderful colors.

Because the seeds germinate slowly, it's always a good idea to soak them in warm water or nick or scrape the hard seed coat before planting them in a pot or in the ground. Keep an eye on the plants as they start to mount their support and redirect or cut back wandering stems. Some types will reseed and can become a nuisance, though seedlings are easy to pull up.

GOOD CHOICES: the classic 'Heavenly Blue' has larger, 6-inch flowers, of sky blue with white throats; 'Scarlett O'Hara' is bright red; intriguing 'Milky Way' has white blooms with ruby-red stripes; Sunrise Mix has white-splashed variations on red, pink, and purple

Passion Flower
Passiflora caerulea
MATURE LENGTH: 15-30 feet
FLOWER COLORS: purple, blue, pink, white
FLOWER SIZE: 4 inches
BLOOM TIME: summer
SOIL: well drained
ZONES: 7-10

A vigorous semitropical vine with remarkable flowers, passion flower can be grown year-round in mild climates and overwintered indoors in a pot elsewhere. The complex flowers splay open to show off delicate outer petals, a boss of colorful filaments, and prominent center stamens. Spanish missionaries to the New World bestowed the common name we use today, citing symbolism in the flower parts to signify Christ's passion.

Passion flower produces loads of flowers all summer long as it mounts fences, arbors, or trellises, holding on with twining tendrils. For best results, site in well-drained soil that is moist or watered regularly. By autumn, the flowers yield to a crop of small, yellow-orange or green, egg-shaped fruits that, while not harmful, don't have much flavor either. Passion vine species are the favored host plants of the gulf fritillary butterfly caterpillar; the plant will recover easily after the caterpillars have finished feeding.

GOOD CHOICES: 'Constance Elliott' has fragrant white blooms; 'Grandiflora', has bigger, 6-inch flowers

Sweet Autumn Clematis

Clematis paniculata (C. dioscoreifolia, C. terniflora)

MATURE LENGTH: 15-20 feet
FLOWER COLORS: white
FLOWER SIZE: 1-1½ inches
BLOOM TIME: midsummer to mid-fall
SOIL: fertile, moist, well drained
ZONES: 5-9

For a good privacy screen on a fence or porch, or for thorough coverage of an arbor, this beautiful vine is ideal. It grows vigorously, high and wide, with ample leaflets of glossy dark green. In the latter part of the summer, it generates great, billowing masses of tiny, fragrant, star-shaped white flowers. These continue well into fall, making a fantastic showing. Decorative, fluffy seedheads then appear, enhancing fall's textural collage and usually persisting into winter.

As with the related, big-flowered clematis, the "head in the sun, feet in the shade" policy applies. So let sweet autumn clematis grow in the sun, but try to shelter or at least mulch the shallow root system.

GOOD CHOICES: the species is lovely, and there are no cultivars to date

Sweet Pea

***Lathyrus* species**

MATURE LENGTH: 6-8 feet
FLOWER COLOR: purple, pink, white, bicolors
FLOWER SIZE: 1½-2 inches
BLOOM TIME: late spring to summer
SOIL: fertile, well drained
ZONES: 5-9

If you haven't grown your own sweet peas before, you are missing out on one of flower gardening's greatest joys. For a little effort at planting time, they reward you handsomely with scads of colorful, sweetly perfumed flowers for weeks. These are delightful in the garden and make for enchanting homegrown bouquets.

Annual sweet peas (*L. odoratus*) are best in areas with cooler summers. Or you can give them an early start by sowing seeds ahead of time in pots indoors. They have a hard seed coat, so soak seeds overnight and nick them with a knife. Or grow the perennial species, *L. latifolius*. Sweet peas attach to supports with grasping tendrils, which appear quickly, so install a support or guiding string at planting time. Pinch tops to encourage strong side growth.

GOOD CHOICES: the Mammoth Early Strain is vigorous, has big flowers on long cutting stems, and starts blooming early; 'Old Spice' is a gorgeous heirloom mix that prospers in warmer climates

VINES AND CLIMBERS

Trumpet Flower
Campsis radicans
MATURE LENGTH: 30 feet
FLOWER COLORS: red, orange
FLOWER SIZE: 2-3 inches
BLOOM TIME: midsummer
SOIL: fertile, moist, well drained
ZONES: 5-9

This is not a vine for the faint-hearted. While it can drape over a small tree or climb any trellis, small or weak ones are soon overwhelmed. Even a stone or brick chimney might not be up to the job. Good places are a freestanding wall, a rock pile, a large tree stump, or an old garden shed.

Midway through the summer, the thickly growing green leaflets and tan stems, which grasp supports via aerial rootlets, are joined by multitudes of bright orange-red trumpet-shaped flowers in clusters at the ends of the stems. The whole garden lights up and hummingbirds flock to them!

Over time, trumpet vine tends to become top-heavy. If you don't intervene and chop it back in early spring, the flowers—and the hummingbirds—will be too high up for you to enjoy them.

GOOD CHOICES: 'Madame Galen' has dark orange-red flower; 'Yellow Trumpet' has yellow flowers

Wisteria
Wisteria species
MATURE LENGTH: 30 feet
FLOWER COLORS: white, pink, violet
FLOWER SIZE: 6-12 inch clusters
BLOOM TIME: spring to summer
SOIL: moist, well drained
ZONES: 5-9

If you want to plant a wisteria, you must choose wisely (*W. floribunda* is more cold hardy than *W. sinensis*) and, often, wait patiently for blooms to appear, because larger, well-established plants are the ones that bloom best. Native wisterias, such as *W. frutescens*, are smaller plants overall, and less aggressive spreaders.

Wisterias look best on arbors or pergolas, sturdy supports where the flowers are able to dangle down from above. Be aware they can pull down a slim trellis and uproot roof shingles. To persuade them to bloom, you can try some or all of the following techniques: grow in full sun, water often and deeply, fertilize throughout the spring and summer, cut out suckers at the base of the plant, and, finally, try root-pruning (ask or hire a landscaper).

GOOD CHOICES: purple-violet *W. floribunda* 'Royal Purple' ('Black Dragon') is spectacular; an outstanding white is *W. sinensis* 'Alba'; *W. frutescens* 'Amethyst Falls' is good for smaller gardens

plant index

cultural index

meet the author

Teri Dunn

Teri Dunn is a freelance writer and editor. She is a former Senior Copy Writer for Jackson & Perkins. Her articles on roses, perennials, water lilies, wildflowers, and other topics have appeared in *Horticulture* magazine, for which she worked for many years as an Associate Editor. Teri is the author of numerous other gardening titles, including *Jackson & Perkins Beautiful Roses Made Easy; Jackson & Perkins Selecting, Growing, and Combining Outstanding Perennials; Potting Places: Creative Ideas for Practical Gardening Workplaces; Cottage Gardens, 600 Essential Plants;* and several books in the popular *100 Favorites* series on roses, perennials, herbs, shade plants, and others. She resides on Cape Ann, Massachusetts, with her husband Shawn and sons Wes and Tristan.